Democracy and Difference

Democracy and Difference

Anne Phillips

Polity Press

The right of Anne Phillips to be identified as author of this work has been asserted in accordance with the Copyright, Designs and Patents Act 1988.

First published in 1993 by Polity Press in association with Blackwell Publishers

Reprinted 2002

Editorial office:
Polity Press
65 Bridge Street
Cambridge CB2 1UR, UK

Marketing and production:
Blackwell Publishers
108 Cowley Road
Oxford OX4 1JF, UK

ISBN 0 7456 1096 X
ISBN 0 7456 1097 8 (pbk)

British Library Cataloguing-in-Publication Data
A CIP catalogue record for this book is available from the British Library.

Typeset in 10 on 12pt Times
by Graphicraft Typesetters Ltd, Hong Kong
Printed in Great Britain by Athenæum Press Ltd, Gateshead, Tyne & Wear

This book is printed on acid-free paper.

Contents

Acknowledgements

I am grateful for permission to reproduce the following essays:

'Fraternity', in *Fabian Essays in Socialist Thought*, ed. Ben Pimlott (London: Heinemann, 1984), pp. 230–41.

'"So What's Wrong with the Individual?" Socialist and Feminist Debates on Equality', in *Socialism and the Limits of Liberalism*, ed. Peter Osborne (London: Verso; New York: New Left Books, 1991), pp. 139–60.

'Universal Pretensions in Political Thought', in *Destabilizing Theory: Contemporary Feminist Debates*, ed. Michèle Barrett and Anne Phillips (Cambridge: Polity; Stanford, CT: Stanford University Press, 1992), pp. 10–30.

'Citizenship and Feminist Theory', in *Citizenship*, ed. Geoff Andrews (London: Lawrence & Wishart, 1991), pp. 76–88.

'Democracy and Difference: Some Problems for Feminist Theory', in *Political Quarterly*, 63, 1 (1992), pp. 79–90.

'Must Feminists Give up on Liberal Democracy?', in *Prospects for Democracy*, special issue of *Political Studies*, ed. David Held, 40 (1992), pp. 68–82.

Most of these are reproduced with only minor revisions designed to edit out repetition or fill in background that had seemed unnecessary at the original time of publication. The main exceptions are 'Citizenship and Feminist Theory', which was originally written to a limit of 5,000 words, and has been extended, and 'Universal Pretensions in Political Thought', which was written partly as an overview of recent feminist political theory and has been revised and reduced. I have tried not to be over-generous to myself in these revisions, and to let earlier – as well as later – imperfections stand.

'The Promise of Democracy' is based on a public lecture given at City of London Polytechnic, March 1992.

'Pluralism, Solidarity and Change' is based on a paper given at Bristol Polytechnic in February 1992, in a seminar series organized by Jeffrey Weeks on the theme of 'Contingency and Solidarity: The Impact of Social Diversity'.

My thanks to David Held at Polity Press, who first suggested that I put together a collection of my essays and has given me much encouragement as well as useful advice; and to Sandy Thatcher at Pennsylvania State University Press, who helped make it a positive pleasure to have two editors working on the job. The essays themselves span a period of nearly ten years, and I will not even attempt to thank the friends who contributed so much through discussion and conversation, comments on early drafts, or responses to the initial publication. I would like, however, to register my intellectual debts to Carole Pateman and Iris Marion Young, whose work has been so important to the development of feminist thinking on democracy and difference.

I am grateful to the Nuffield Foundation, which provided me with a Social Science Research Fellowship in 1992–3 to work on issues of democracy and group representation. The introduction and final essay were completed during the first stages of this project, which grew out of the theoretical explorations that are represented in this volume. Work on earlier essays was made easier by the generous research time allowed me by London Guildhall University, which sheltered me from some of the more unhappy consequences of rapidly rising student numbers.

My thanks, finally, to Ciaran Driver, who has always been willing to discuss thorny issues of democracy and gets little in return when it comes to discussing economics; and to my sons Declan and Anthony, for putting up (if not without protest) with the irritability and self-obsession that often accompanies writing.

Introduction

There are two stories of democracy that circulate today, and, like most tales of political endeavour, they allow us to choose between a happy ending and a future that is still unresolved. Both stories imply progression, and both regard the current moment as in some sense exceptional. The first tells of a long march of history from the early democracies of the Greek city states, through the initially non-democratic nation states and empires of Europe, and out into the liberal, representative democracy that is the appropriate form for today. In this tale, most of the twentieth century appears as a horrifying diversion. Liberal democracy was challenged on the one side by the authoritarian nationalism of fascist regimes, which set loyalty to the nation above citizen rights and physically eliminated unwanted communities, and on the other side by the repressive totalitarianism of communist regimes, which set the rhetoric of equality above the accountability of government and also eliminated millions of people. In the less troubled heartlands of liberal democracy, malcontents continued to appeal to outdated notions of direct democracy as their alternative to representation, or insisted that political rights were empty when superimposed on economic inequality. Fortunately for us, the story goes on, these alternatives have been roundly defeated. Liberal democracy may not yet be the dominant political arrangement in the world's nations, but it has at last won the battle of ideas. All kinds of adjustments are still possible or desirable, but the basic outlines of the appropriate democracy are finally and firmly in place.[1]

The second story tells it differently, and takes up the tale at a different point. Skimming rather rapidly through the earlier chapters, it pauses mainly to note the extensive prohibitions that have kept so many people out of the political community, up to and including much of the twentieth century. No period, either in the past or the present, then serves as a model for democracy; and all the battles between direct and representative, liberal and socialist, protective and consensual democracy appear as a sub-text to the central drama, which only now begins to unfold. As universal suffrage is almost universally adopted, the main interest in this story lies in the continuing exclusions from substantial citizenship, and the problems that are associated with equality in the context of difference. It is noted, for example, that women can now vote on official parity with men, but that this has only mildly dented the masculine political dominance. Jews, Catholics and Muslims usually enjoy full civil and political rights, but religious minorities often feel excluded from their country's political culture. Most democracies are now a mosaic of different cultural and ethnic groups, but the homogenizing myths of country or nation mean that only some of these groups will feel they are full members of the political community. How are democracies to deal with divisions by gender or ethnicity or religion or race, and the way these impinge on political equality? What meaning can we give to the political community when so many groups feel themselves outside it? How can democracies deliver on equality while accommodating and indeed welcoming difference? The questions then turn on the kind of politics that can recognize and legitimate group difference while resisting fragmentation into discrete and local identities, and the kind of solidarity that becomes possible if we give up on the presumption of an undifferentiated humanity. The story is left deliberately open-ended, but with a strong sense that these are the issues that will dominate the future. There is reference back to some of the earlier explorations of democracy in a plural society, as in the consociational democracies of Western Europe. But, most typically, there is reference forward to the urgency with which these issues are now posed: in the continuing phenomenon of a second-class citizenship for women; in the internal and persistently racial politics of the United States of America; in the dissolution of the Soviet Union; or in the destructive nationalisms of Central Europe.

The first story has so far reached the wider audience, but the more interesting point is that the two tales deal in such different kinds of material. As recently as ten years ago, the first was countered by something that was almost its mirror image – except, that is, in the condemnation of fascism, one point on which all democrats could agree. Beyond that, positions on democracy fell broadly into two schools of thought.

There were those who supported liberal democracy and those who regarded it as an impoverished and inadequate form; the second group offered a far more positive reading of the practices of ancient democracy or the skirmishes of recent decades. There were important differences of emphasis here, most markedly a contrast between European and American debates. Radical democracy inside Europe has been more consistently influenced by a socialist or social-democratic tradition, and has homed in on the tensions between political equality and economic subordination, arguing that democracy is incomplete until it addresses social and economic concerns. Radical democracy inside the USA has drawn more of its inspiration from the republican ideals that informed the founding of the nation, and has focused on the apathy and failures of participation that mar contemporary democratic regimes. But, in either case, there was a direct challenge to the story as told by defenders of liberal democracy: there were critics and supporters, and the strengths or weaknesses of liberal democracy provided the central axis of debate.

This pattern of alignment has been clouded by the subsequent crisis in alternatives to liberal democracy, a crisis that is evidenced not only in the collapse of self-styled socialist or communist governments, but in the wider failure of confidence in direct participation and substantial equality. It is not that radicals have given up the ghost; there are plenty of us still around who challenge the complacencies of democracy today. But the fear of appearing naive is much stronger than it was in the heady days of what we sometimes termed a revolution (remember student revolution? women's liberation? black power? these dramatic descriptions now seem millennia away from the sober realities of the 1990s). The support group has dissolved and, along with it, the confidence in staking out something different. I have been struck by the number of occasions in recent conferences or seminars when exponents of a more radical vision of democracy were asked to say whether this meant they 'rejected' liberal democracy – and none of them has been comfortable with this description. No one is happy with the simpler divisions of 'for' or 'against'; no one wants to be tainted by the utopianism of earlier decades. This resolute realignment may well signal a retreat from democracy's grander promise, but it also opens up to discussion newer questions associated with democracy and group difference.

Particularly notable in this transition is the movement away from class as the major tool of political analysis. Despite the contrast between American and European discussions, the issues of class still provided much of the content in twentieth-century debates on democracy. Attention was directed to the substantive conditions necessary to fulfil the promise of political equality (whether such equality is compatible with the market economy); to the appropriate scope of democratic decision-making (whether it should be extended, for example, to the workplace or the firm); and to the tension between an individualist politics of rights and a more collectivist notion of the common good. The subsequent broadening out from class to gender, race, or ethnicity has changed the terms more dramatically than was initially expected, and what at first looked like an addition soon altered the very framework of debate.

As long as class was considered the pre-eminent group difference, arguments divided relatively neatly between the liberal position which sought to discount differences of class and the socialist position which aimed at their elimination. Once attention shifted to other forms of group difference that were not so amenable to erasure, it became inappropriate to regard these as always and inevitably a problem. In 1970, Shulamith Firestone made a valiant effort towards eliminating sexual difference by visualizing a cybernetic communism that would free women from the tyranny of reproduction and produce children through artificial means.[2] A couple of years earlier, I was in a school-room discussion that anticipated the ending of racial conflict and difference through a few generations of world intermarriage that would eradicate variations in the colour of our skin. These now seem like absurd hangovers from the paradigm of class: people still locked within a language of elimination, a notion that equality becomes possible only when the differences have finally gone. Had there been any black pupils in my class of 68, this presumption might already have been questioned (and the fact that I remember it so clearly suggests that even at the time it sounded rather odd). Certainly the Firestone scenario remained exceptional even in the wilder fantasies of the 1970s, and it soon entered into the demonology of feminism, to be repudiated by conservatives and radicals alike.[3] The problems of class difference and inequality had lent themselves to strategies of elimination or transcendence. Those of gender or ethnicity or sexuality or religion cried out for an alternative approach.

The essays brought together in this collection were written between the years 1984 to 1992, thus precisely over the period in which debates over democracy shifted and perceptions of difference changed. What unites them is a conviction that we must give up on the yearning for an undifferentiated unity as the basis for democratic politics. But what also unifies them is a sense of the dangers in abandoning the aspirations towards universality: the risks of declining into an individualist politics of self-interest; of reinforcing a patchwork of local identities from which people can speak only to their immediate group; or of forgetting the continued salience of class. The collection is inspired, that is, by a vision of democracy *through* difference; a politics that neither denies nor capitulates to the particularity of group identity.

The important backdrop to the collection is that all the essays were written in the context of a crisis in radical politics. They reflect the revision and, more recently, the collapse of Marxism; the growing unease with the universalizing pretensions of Enlightenment rationality; the accommodation with a pluralism that used to be viewed as apologetics for the status quo. The relationship between these three developments is not straightforward, but in each instance feminism played a central role. Feminists took the lead in querying the analysis and indeed the goals of the socialist tradition, laying bare the masculine presumption that took class as the fundamental axis of social oppression, and then compounded this limitation by equating the working class with manual men. Feminists built on such critiques to query what has seemed an endless range of phony universals, and, in the process of writing women into humanity, the working class, the citizen, the individual, have arrived at a more damning indictment of universalizing theory as a homogenizing and exclusionary force. Women were seen as pushed to the margins – in theory as much as in life – and, in exploring the altern-atives to this, feminists have associated themselves with a new, more radical, pluralism that actively celebrates heterogeneity and difference.

For most feminists, these movements have been viewed in a positive rather than a negative light, and we have tended to see ourselves as the bearers of a more thorough-going radicalism that breaks through the ossified structures of previous centuries or decades. This confidence is perhaps particularly marked in the earlier essays. The 1980s was a time of major revision and development in socialist thought, when feminists could claim for themselves a dual role as critic and reviver of the socialist tradition, and could contrast the sorry retreats of an older socialism with the advances that feminists had made. In the course of this decade, the meaning of socialism became so problematic that many found themselves shifting towards the rougher approximation of 'radical' politics instead. Three of the essays in this collection ('Fraternity', 'So What's Wrong with the Individual?', 'Citizenship and Feminist Theory') were written in what was a familiar context to British socialist feminists

through the 1970s and 1980s: explorations of feminism in its relationship to socialism that employ feminism as the more thorough-going
critique. Later essays move the ground of discussion towards what I still
see as the vaguer context of radicalism. Two of these ('Must Feminists
Give up on Liberal Democracy?' and 'Pluralism, Solidarity and Change')
then reflect consciously on what this movement implies.

The changing context is expressed in a mounting sense of the difficulties democrats face, for, as all around seems to conspire to dislodge
ancient certainties, the tearing down of the old has so far outstripped
the process of reconstruction. We are left with more questions than
answers – and, though I keep telling myself that it is better to be without answers than to cling to the ones that were wrong, it is hard to avoid
the occasional moment of doubt. It has in that sense proved a daunting
experience to re-read these separate essays as part of a unified whole –
not so much because I contradict myself or substantially change my
position (I almost wish this were so), but because I seem to circle with
ever-increasing anxiety around the same set of questions, trying to hold
together what I half fear are incompatible ends. Prominent among the
worries are my sense that the universality that flattens out difference
was none the less a great inspiration to progressive politics and thought,
and that the heterogeneity which welcomes variation can carry with it
a disturbing fragmentation and closure. Less explicit, but never far from
the surface, is a feeling that I have not yet come to terms with my
starting point in a socialist tradition.

My socialism predated my feminism and, in a common enough traject-
ory for British feminists, it set much of the framework within which my
feminism first developed. The simplest indicator of this is the importance I attached to the relationship between class and gender, and the
way this influenced both my understanding of women's oppression and
my perceptions of where women's politics might go. I saw feminism as
challenging blind spots in the Marxist and socialist traditions, querying
the theoretical dominance of relations of production as well as the
political dominance of men. This preoccupation confirmed the vitality
of feminist theory and politics, but it also controlled this energy by
sending it through pre-established channels. In the 1970s, for example,
British Marxist-feminists got hung up on a contrast between relations of
production and relations of reproduction, hoping that this would prove
the way towards a more satisfactory materialism; they found themselves
pushed into an over-sharp dichotomy between socialist and radical
feminism, which temporarily blocked their appreciation of the new issues

raised in the radical camp; and through their fixation on the interplay between capitalism and patriarchy they took much longer than they should have done to recognize questions of ethnicity and race. Socialist-feminists also found themselves hampered in their understanding of the relationship between liberalism and feminism, tending to criticize liberalism on socialist rather than feminist grounds.

By the end of the 1970s, the hyphen that joined socialism to feminism was beginning to disappear. A number of British feminists started to describe themselves as socialists *and* feminists, thereby signalling their sense that these two projects might not lend themselves to any more intimate connection. Others quietly dropped the socialist reference point, finding it had outlived its relevance. Particularly striking here was the ease with which previous preoccupations fell away. It was not that the problems in what Heidi Hartmann had termed 'the unhappy marriage of marxism and feminism' were resolved,[4] or that the relationship between capitalism and patriarchy was finally settled.[5] More typically, feminist thinking just moved off in a different direction. People stopped talking in terms of capitalism and patriarchy, and developed an alternative codification of feminist arguments around the notions of equality and difference. What Michèle Barrett has called the 'turn to culture'[6] shifted feminist enthusiasms from broadly materialist analysis in the fields of economics, sociology or anthropology towards work in literary criticism, cultural studies or philosophy. The explosion of feminist political theory (mainly a phenomenon of the 1980s and 1990s) left behind the older triad of liberalism, socialism and feminism to develop a more explicitly feminist appraisal of the principles of liberal and humanist thought. In none of these developments was there a significant settling of previous disputes. It was as if earlier debates had shunted themselves into a forlorn and deserted siding. Later journeys set off from a different station.

One worry with this is that lacking a more explicit settlement of accounts it becomes possible to evade responsibility for deciding which things most matter. Feminist theory 1970s-style was very much concerned with questions of causation, with working out which elements had been most fundamental in producing and sustaining women's oppression and which ones were first candidates for change. Now that 'fundamental' has become such a dirty word (arousing images of religious fundamentalism on the one side, and reminding us of the dangers of philosophical foundationalism on the other), we are loath to carry on in this vein. But the growing attachment to a language of difference may then block consideration of the continuing inequities of class, or, as sometimes seems more likely, encourage a jumbling of different kinds of differences with no attempt at distinction. When we draw up our rainbow coalitions of oppressed and marginalized groups, for example, there is something equally jarring whether class is omitted or included. In the first instance, it seems perverse to leave out one of the major sources of social division – to focus on race or gender or sexuality or religion but keep silent on the inequities of class. But if we do slip 'working-class people' into a list that spans women, black people, disabled people, lesbians, gay men, that too rings strangely in my ears.[7] There are important questions still to be resolved in the relationship between earlier and current debates; and to the extent that they share in a fashionable change of direction, these essays do not resolve them.

The original point of departure is indicated in the first essay in the collection, which draws on the experience of the contemporary women's movement to query socialist 'fraternity'. The most obvious problem with fraternity is that brothers have to be male: as translated into a model for socialist solidarity, this is a language that celebrates male unity while excluding women from its scope. The slippage has proved more than linguistic, for, in its development from the radicalism of the French Revolution into the socialism of nineteenth- and twentieth-century labour movements, fraternity came to embody a notion of solidarity that was best expressed in an exclusionary male-bonding. So far, so much past history: the central point I make is that we must resist nostalgia for what is now ebbing away. Instead of bemoaning the loss of older communities or traditional solidarities, we should take this opportunity to refuse the false fraternity (and indeed the equally deceptive sisterhood) that constrains us to a family likeness. We should release ourselves from the burden of an undifferentiated unity, and no longer act as if the only solidarity worth its name is the one that unites through every aspect of existence. It is not, that is, a matter of redefining solidarity or community so that it loses its masculine resonance and embraces all of us alike. The greater challenge is to come to terms with a complex unity constructed out of different and potentially conflicting solidarities, a unity that is then fragile and perhaps always and inevitably incomplete.

The essay thus builds on feminist understanding of heterogeneity to query the traditional solidarities of labour and socialist movements, and encourages a more confident attitude towards the weakening of these masculine bonds. I wrote, however, more confidently than I felt, and almost immediately found myself drawn into a politics that seemed at odds with my formal position. The time of publication was a difficult one for British radicals, for it coincided with a lengthy strike by the National Union of Mineworkers over major pit closures that threatened to destroy the livelihood of entire communities. For many socialists (myself included), this strike seemed a last line of defence against a government overtly dedicated to destroying the power of trade unions, and one that demanded wholehearted support. For many feminists (again myself included) it became a particularly pressing rallying ground when women in the mining communities formed their own autonomous organization to publicize and maintain the strike, forging an exuberant politics of working-class women that most feminists were keen to endorse.

The combination of events generated considerable political confusion, and I well remember my own sense of disorientation. Here was a strike that appeared in retrospect as the last stand of a dying tradition. Coal mining in Britain is a wholly masculine preserve (guaranteed as such by one hundred and fifty years of protective legislation), and its trade union traditions could serve as a textbook example of the exclusionary fraternity of working-class men. This alone made my support for the strike rather suspect, for had I not argued against nostalgia for solidarities such as these? More poignantly still, the 1984 strike had been called without a ballot of union members, and it soon became a symbolic battleground over which socialists refined their positions on democracy. In the older framework of liberal versus socialist democracy, socialists had paid too little attention to the precise mechanisms of democratic accountability, tending to emphasize structural inequalities in class power at the expense of internal organizational democracy. But in the often anguished and bitter debates over the 1984 strike, many refused to support a cause that was not legitimated by a democratic ballot. The formation of Women Against Pit Closures provided many feminists with a way out of this crisis of alignment; but the relief was only temporary, and in the aftermath of the (defeated) strike, the reassessment carried on apace.[8]

The second essay in this collection was written several years later, when the convergence of liberal and socialist thinking had moved significantly on. Socialist recuperation of the individual has been a particularly prominent element in this. The abstractions of the individual used to be a major source of complaint against the liberal tradition, which was said to disregard the contingencies of social existence to deal only in the essential equality of all individuals, and to elevate a self-protective individualism into the ultimate in human freedom. Communitarian theorists have since carried this debate into the heartlands of liberal thinking, taking issue with the 'unencumbered self' as a sociological and a philosophical absurdity, and resurrecting more classical notions of the community as the context from which all freedoms derive their meaning. At the same time, however, there was a major rewriting of Marxist socialism to ground it in impeccably individualist assumptions: G. A. Cohen's *Karl Marx's Theory of History* was an early example of this, to be followed in the 1980s by John Roemer's reworking of Marx's theory of exploitation and Jon Elster's *tour de force* in *Making Sense of Marx.*[9] This philosophical reappraisal of the groundings of historical materialism combined with an equally energetic reassessment of the language of rights to change the parameters between liberal and socialist thought. With Marxists grounding their analyses in rational choice and socialists looking to John Rawls for inspiration, it was hard to know who or what was liberal, and where the difference with socialism lay.

What struck me most forcibly at the time was the way these developments reversed the respective positions of socialism and feminism. Not too long ago, it was feminism that was the more ambivalently disposed towards the liberal tradition, with socialism more clearly antagonistic. But where socialists had once contested what they saw as the false abstractions of the individual or citizen or consumer, they now seemed to be reclaiming the individual as both the beginning and the end of their project. And where feminists had once drawn much of their inspiration from liberal notions of the free and autonomous individual, they were now developing a sharper critique. Many recent feminists have taken issue with the individual of liberal philosophy, focusing not so much on its 'empty' abstractions as on its all too solidly masculine content. Most notably, perhaps, Carole Pateman has built on C. B. Macpherson's account of possessive individualism to argue that the individual of liberal philosophy is a man in gender-free guise, a sexual master who possesses his body and thus self, who must be constrained in his attempts to possess others.[10] Contemporary ideals of both freedom and individuality are too much tainted by this masculine presence, and, rather than seeking out a better – because more thoroughly disembodied – abstraction, we would be well advised to consider the individual as both women and men.

In reviewing this recent transposition, the essay employs feminist arguments to resurrect an earlier socialist distrust of abstraction, and relies on the newer issues of feminism to halt an over-enthusiastic socialist retreat. To this extent, it remains within that older (and perhaps particularly British) framework in which feminists could conceive themselves as radicalizing and revitalizing a potentially moribund but still socialist tradition. The argument is already shifting, however, towards questions more intrinsic to democracy and difference. What most troubles me in this essay is how far we should go in challenging abstraction, and I register my concern over the sharper contrasts between (male) abstraction and (female) specificity that have characterized much recent feminist debate. The obvious example here – and this recurs as a reference point in later essays – is Carol Gilligan's work contrasting the ethic of rights and the ethic of responsibility, which has been widely (though I think wrongly) interpreted as an attack on impartiality and fairness in the name of a more contextualized notion of care.

It is, I note, 'one of the paradoxes of contemporary feminist writing that so much of it identifies false oppositions, dualisms or dichotomies as the characteristics of orthodox, masculine thought, and yet so much of it reads like a straightforward reversal of what previous writers have said' (p. 52). Translated into the issues surrounding democracy and difference, these false dichotomies can encourage a wholesale rejection of the universalisms of humanity, and what then begins to preoccupy me is what we may be risking in the course of this critique. These questions are pushed further in 'Universal Pretensions in Political Thought', which I include here (though it says little directly on democracy) as an overview of these explorations both in feminist and notfeminist thought.

A number of writers have noted the parallels between feminist challenges to universalizing theory and the more mainstream arguments of communitarian or post-modern critics, and in drawing attention to this overlap I stress the common criticism both developments have provoked. 'In each case', I note, 'the move away from grand theory and towards a more specific, historically grounded, or else gendered, account, has laid itself open to complaints of incipient conservatism' (p. 58). A central issue here is whether critical theory is possible without some external reference point against which to measure the inadequacies of our time. What is it that enables us to get sufficiently 'outside' existing conditions or presumptions in order to question their force? At a minimum, it is the sense that things do not fit: that there is a contradiction, for example, between the declared principles of a particular society and its practices towards certain groups, or that the principles judged appropriate in the public sphere are disregarded in the practices of the private. The first was the basis on which John Stuart Mill attacked the subordination of women, arguing that it was inconsistent not to apply to women the dominant principle of modern society, which he took as the notion that what individuals do with their lives should be decided by competition and not birth. The second has played a crucial role in both socialist and feminist judgements on the limitations of liberal democracy. Neither of these strategies has depended on reference to an external or universal standard, but both of them call for some measure of connection between things previously thought of as separate.

This suggests that we can manage well enough without a bank of timeless truths against which to judge each society's imperfections, but that we do need some capacity for connecting one kind of experience with another. The starker oppositions between universality and difference potentially hinder this, for they could encourage a celebration of difference that blocks comparison and subsequently alliance. I argue, however, that there is little in the work of contemporary feminists that would justify this worrying conclusion, and that even those who most directly challenge the universalisms of traditional political or moral thought are weaving a careful way between the demands of the particular and the general.

The relationship between these more general debates and the project of a radical democracy is then the explicit focus of subsequent essays. 'Citizenship and Feminist Theory' is written in the context of British rediscoveries of the citizen as a focus for radical renewal, and, as in the earlier essay on the individual, I note the space opening up between a deliberately abstracted language of citizenship and a feminist insistence on difference. Much of the work in this field is developing on the broad terrain of social policy, where issues of gender are transforming the analysis of citizen rights or responsibilities, and where new notions of social citizenship are emerging that build on a feminist analysis of care.[11] My own preoccupations centre around more directly political questions, and I look to the rather different discourse of citizenship that has informed debate in the USA.

It is worth returning here to the two kinds of challenges to liberal democracy that I identified with European and American traditions. The first focuses on the classically liberal separation between public and private spheres, and notes the contradictions that have emerged between the public realm of political equality and the private realm of continuing economic and social subordination. One common strategy, from this perspective, is to call for a far-reaching extension of democracy into all those so-called private spheres: thus to argue, from a conventionally socialist direction, for workers' control in factories; from a more 1960s' inspired participationism, for student control and neighbourhood control, and decentralization of all decisions; and from a feminist direction, for the democratization of family and household and everyday life. The failures of democracy are then perceived in terms of the false separation between public and private, and the radicalism of democracy is associated with its being spread more fully around.

The other critique associated with radical democracy in the United States has stressed the declining significance of the public sphere. In a tradition inspired by classical notions of republican duty and citizenship, and much influenced by the work of Hannah Arendt, many American writers have expressed their near despair at the parochialism and self-interest and the grasping pressure-group politics that characterizes so much of democracy today. From this perspective, the micropolitics of grassroots democracy is not likely to prove the solution: as Sheldon Wolin puts it in a 1982 essay, 'the localism that is the strength of grassroots organizations is also their limitation.'[12] When so many of the problems that face us are general in nature and require a vision that looks beyond what is local, the prospects for a better democracy lie not in dissolving distinctions between public and private but more actively revitalizing the public sphere.

The issues associated with group difference find easier access to the first alternative than the second, but this only highlights the dangers of travelling exclusively down this road. As Mary Dietz argues in a number of important essays, it is in the nature of democratic politics that we have to engage with others as our political equals, and this process cannot even begin if we remain too exclusively defined by our identities as teachers or mothers or workers or sisters. Citizenship, she argues, is about transformation, and it involves some process of separation from the concerns of our more immediate sphere. But this then seems at odds with the insights feminists have developed from their critique of universal pretensions. In her assessment of Benjamin Barber's *Strong Democracy*, for example, Iris Marion Young queries the value he attaches to transcendence and the way he equates democratic citizenship with an ability to rethink initial prejudices and go beyond immediate concerns.[13] She sees this appeal to an impartial or general perspective as something that will enhance the dominance of already dominant groups, and argues that the emphasis placed on transcendence will silence the voices of those who are more marginal. If this criticism is correct, how then can we retain the positive insights of republican democracy, with its damning indictment of pressure group politics and its powerful vision of common concerns, while still exposing group difference and inequality and ensuring that all voices are accorded equal weight? The resolution, I suggest, lies somewhere in the gap between transformation and transcendence: the first rightly stressing the limits of localized and specific identities, but the latter pursuing this to the point of jettisoning all group differences and concerns.

My essay on 'Democracy and Difference' represents a hardening of my position on this. I turn to the policy proposals arising out of Iris Young's critique of transcendence – a variety of procedures that will secure the specific representation of oppressed groups – and I argue that this is not the route to take. The false abstractions of citizenship must indeed be challenged, as must the extraordinary under-representation of women and ethnic minority citizens inside our political assemblies, and I am unambiguously in favour of party quota systems as a way of achieving more equal political representation. But the more specific representation of groups founders on the difficulties of establishing which group is most pertinent to anyone's political identity, the dangers of freezing identities in a way that blocks wider solidarities, and the almost impossible tasks of making group 'representatives' accountable to 'their' group. The problems of democracy and difference are not resolved through group representation.

'Must Feminists Give up on Liberal Democracy?' provides both an overview of where feminists have got to in the development of a democratic agenda, and an explicit reassessment of what this means in the contemporary political climate. Part of the background to this lies in the responses to my book *Engendering Democracy*, which was published in the preceding year. As the title suggests, this set out to explore the difference feminism makes to our understanding of democracy, and I had embarked on the project with the expectation of writing a specifically feminist critique of liberal democracy. As usual, things did not turn out exactly to plan. In pursuing the liberal separation between public and private spheres, I found my criticisms moderated by a sense that some kind of distinction remained necessary; in exploring problems associated with participatory democracy (as confirmed by much of the experience of the contemporary women's movement) I found myself reaching a closer accommodation than I had expected with liberal notions of representation; in identifying the difficulties feminism raises for the major alternatives to liberal democracy, I became rather even-handed in my assessment of liberal democracy and its critics. Even so, I was somewhat taken aback by my editor's perception of the book as almost a defence of liberal democracy and a subsequent book review that noted my 'liberal caution'.[14] What precipitated the final form of this essay was a remark by David Beetham (at the conference in which the first draft was discussed) to the effect that he agreed with much of the argument of *Engendering Democracy* but did not see why it had to be put in the framework of rejecting liberal democracy. The article represents my attempt at sorting this out, so that it serves both as an abbreviated version of some of the key arguments from *Engendering Democracy* and as a later reformulation of these as not meaning we must give up on liberal democracy.

That said, it can also be read, in combination with the final two essays, as an assertion of the continuing importance of participation. The standard liberal complaint against devotees of a more participatory democracy is that voting is the only form of political participation that can be regarded as genuinely egalitarian. All more demanding forms of participation end up as the preserve of an unrepresentative minority: the 'politically active' with their unusual appetite for meetings. As Giovanni Sartori has argued, a more participatory democracy can end up as a more elitist politics, in which 'the few do better and count for more, than the passive, inert, apathetic, nonparticipant many.'[15] This complaint is often reinforced by a suggestion that activists follow an agenda peculiar to themselves, and that their preoccupations bear no relation to the preferences of those who are inactive. Even if we reject this accusation (which is often at odds with the findings of empirical studies) there remains an important point for anyone concerned with democracy. Indeed much of my resistance to proposals for group representation stems from an anticipation of self-selecting and unrepresentative elites who will escape mechanisms of democratic accountability. Anyone who has been involved in radical politics will know the difficulties in ensuring that active participation is also widely based, and these difficulties are further confirmed when approached from a feminist direction. As long as the sexual distribution of labour allocates to women the main responsibility for caring for others, the time left over for political engagement will necessarily be reduced. Those involved in the women's liberation movement threw themselves into an enthusiastically engaged democracy – but, given the constraints on women's time, it was in some ways astonishing that feminists sought out the most demanding of democratic forms.

To set against this, I note the major counter-arguments to minimalist democracy, which turn on the necessity for transformation. Initially at least, this is a different point from that made by Mary Dietz in her discussion of citizenship: not so much the transformation from our identities as workers or mothers to our more general citizen role, as an even earlier process of transformation in which we identify our needs and concerns. Contemporary feminism has placed much of its emphasis on the cultural relations through which women come to view themselves and their lives, and, though few feminists would now employ the discredited language of 'false consciousness', nearly all will agree that women's perceptions of themselves and their interests are contradictory or unstable. One implication is that the kind of democracy that simply registers existing preferences or interests (quintessentially through the procedures of casting an occasional vote) cannot deal adequately with women's concerns. It is only through the more time-consuming procedures of meeting and discussing and deciding that we can explore our sense of oppression and identify the changes we most need. To this extent, there is no going back from the grander ideals of active participation, even when the reservations over time and degrees of commitment are taken more fully into account.

'The Promise of Democracy' was written as an inaugural professorial lecture for an audience expected to be largely indifferent to either feminism or participatory democracy; and, like the previous essay, it speaks from the political context of the early 1990s, when liberal democracy is so widely perceived as having captured the dominant ground. Temporarily sidestepping the issue of participation, I focus on the more recent promise of democratic equality, noting how this has displaced the older ideals of active participation in the pursuit of common concerns. The promise, I argue, is very far from fulfilled, and particularly so when we consider the group differences in a plural society. I go back to the alternative scenarios offered in 'Democracy and Difference': the choice between equalizing our political access as individual members of disadvantaged groups and representing what are specifically group identities and concerns. The first scenario, I argue, is already pretty radical, for it involves substantial social intervention to remove the obstacles to equal participation, and can combine this with quota systems to ensure a genuine equality of outcome. It still falls short, however, of delivering the conditions under which disadvantaged or marginalized groups can press specifically group concerns, and by this point I have arrived at a distinction between majority and minority groups. Since women constitute half of every society, their representation can be quite adequately encompassed within the first scenario, for, once the necessary social and political reforms achieve parity of political representation, women will then make up half of any decision-making body. The more difficult problems arise in delivering political equality to minority groups – groups, that is, who by virtue of their language or religion or ethnicity or nation of origin form a numerical minority. Parity of representation hardly seems sufficient in such a context, for it may deliver too token a presence to change the political agenda.[16] Additional and specifically group representation seems to creep back onto the programme.

In the final essay on 'Pluralism, Solidarity and Change', I reach a clearer resolution of these issues. I focus here on the differences between the old and the new pluralisms, arguing that exponents of the latter face a problem that barely figures for theorists of the former. The new pluralism arises out of a radical tradition that sets its sight on future change. Because of this, it cannot rest content with a live and let live toleration that just enjoins each group to get on with its own private affairs. But, inspired as it is by a far-reaching egalitarianism that wants to empower currently disadvantaged groups, it is also more likely than the older pluralism to validate an exclusive and fragmented politics of identity that blocks the development of wider solidarity. The conventional pluralism of much twentieth-century political science deals with interest rather than identity groups, thus with groups that overlap in their membership, and are organized around issues that may be only moderately felt. Such groups may more happily reach accommodation with those pressing alternative concerns. Radical pluralism, by contrast, focuses on groups that are defined by a common experience of exclusion or oppression, thus on identities that are often secured in direct opposition to some 'other'. The intensity of identity politics is less amenable to a politics of accommodation or compromise, and is far more likely to encourage fragmentation or mutual hostility.

Consociationalism has been the main exception to the orthodox political science emphasis on interest rather than identity groups, but, even at its best, it provides an argument for fairer distribution rather than a politics of transformation and change. Consociationalism is driven by the requirements of political stability, and it derives from this its case for a fairer distribution of power and resources between a plurality of social groups. It restricts itself, however, to such groups as have already revealed themselves in the formation of separate political parties; it accepts as more or less inevitable the continuing hostilities between such groups; and, where it anticipates inter-group communication, it sees this as an exclusively elite affair. Such a solution to the problems of democracy and difference is not going to appeal to radical democrats, who will hardly warm to a politics in which competing groups secure their equality behind ever higher barriers of mutual distrust and only communicate via their respective elites. This suggests that equality in power or resources can only be part of the answer, and must combine with the more engaged and participatory politics that enhances communication between different groups. If democracies are to practise some kind of affirmative action in the realm of political representation – some mechanism, that is, for guaranteeing equality between different groups – this puts a higher premium than ever on increasing political engagement. Failing this, people may well entrench themselves behind barriers of mutual resentment, which will soon defeat the egalitarian aims.

While any call for greater political participation and engagement risks being labelled utopian or unreal, the issues posed here are of immediate pertinence to contemporary political events. In a particularly disturbing analysis of recent American politics, for example, Thomas and Mary Edsall have argued that much of the 1980s' crisis in political support for the Democratic Party stemmed from a growing association in the minds of voters between Democratic liberalism and being soft on blacks.[17] A new elite displaced big business as the focus of anti-establishment resentment: an elite culled from the assorted ranks of feminists, civil rights leaders, liberal judges, and others who spoke for excluded or marginalized groups. Republican ideologues, they argue, worked hard to foster this resentment, repackaging a range of post-war 'liberal' policies as intrusive and expensive programmes paid for by the white working class.

> In particular, busing, affirmative action, and much of the rights revolution in behalf of criminal defendants, prisoners, homosexuals, welfare recipients, and a host of other previously marginalized groups have, for many voters, converted the government from ally to adversary. The simultaneous increase, over the past two and a half decades, in crime, welfare dependency, illegitimacy, and educational failure have established in the minds of many voters a numbing array of 'costs' – perceived and real – of liberalism.[18]

The very notion of fairness, they suggest, became associated with 'fairness to minorities', and, instead of serving as a rallying cry against the growing disparity of income between rich and poor, helped deliver a significant tranche of working-class support to the Republican Party.

In both the UK and the USA, the gap between rich and poor widened substantially in the course of the 1980s, as high levels of unemployment became endemic and tax cuts favoured those who were already better off. In both cases, however, the party with the most claim to represent the poor and the working class (the Labour Party in Britain, the Democrats in the USA) proved incapable of seizing the political advantage. The implication of the Edsalls' analysis is that, in America at least, this paralysis in the face of growing material inequality stemmed from a refusal to consider the limits of what the electorate would support. Secure in the confidence that their policies were more inherently progressive, liberal reformers refused to heed the voices of those white manual workers who felt themselves at the sharp edge of affirmative action programmes. They paid the price in losing five out of six presidential elections.

The politician's response to this is simply to evacuate the field. The election of Bill Clinton as the first Democratic president since Jimmy Carter might seem to invalidate the Edsall analysis – except that the Democrats reformed themselves during the 1992 campaign on the middle ground of middle America, facing down what they saw as the more disruptive versions of black politics, and proposing a new approach to welfare which would require recipients to accept training or work. The British Labour Party has never been associated with particularly radical programmes on gender or race, but, in throwing off a parallel identification with supposedly over-powerful unions, it has also strained every muscle to recapture the middle ground. In both cases, the party responds to criticism by jettisoning divisive or disruptive baggage, and, while this may slow down the accumulation of resentment against trade unionists or minority groups, it does little to deal with genuine disparities in power. The other alternative is to acknowledge the misapprehensions and conflicts that divide one group from another, and encourage more engagement and debate. Equality cannot be detached from participation, for egalitarian initiatives are all too likely to founder unless linked to better communication between social groups.

Jean Leca has talked of the way that different cultural groups come to communicate with one another only with the 'deafness of resentment',[19] but this is not something restricted to those groups who feel themselves excluded from the dominant political community. As the American experience indicates, the deafness is just as likely to descend on people who see their marginal advantages under threat. This is a phenomenon that feeds on misapprehension and non-communication, and no amount of social engineering by enlightened reformers can be guaranteed to dissolve resentment. If the requirements of equality were transparent, these problems might not arise. All citizens might then grasp immediately what justice demanded and approve whatever mechanisms are suggested for achieving the desired end. But since the requirements of equality are far from obvious – this is particularly so when we are talking of equality between people who remain different – no government can presume the automatic approval of its people to whatever measures it might propose. People have to be drawn into a fuller appreciation of different needs and concerns and priorities, and there is no substitute for political engagement as the process through which this occurs.

There are three forces that can generate a sense of belonging to the same community. One of these is a similarity in being, and my starting point in this collection of essays is that this option is no longer available. We can no longer construct a version of the political community that is premised on us having the same experience – all men together, all English together, all white together, and so on. Or, more precisely, people can still seek out a community based on sameness, but those who do so have to resort either to the brutalities of 'ethnic cleansing', or to the more commonplace dishonesty of offering us all citizenship and then saying we can enjoy it only when we become like somebody else. Homogeneity was never, in my opinion, a desirable basis for a community; but trying to stick with it today requires considerable deception and distortion.

The second force is economic growth and development, which can sometimes deliver a sufficiently wide basis of material well-being to encourage a shared sense of belonging. There have been important moments like this, but none in recent years; in the context of what seems like global recession, there is little immediate prospect of it. Growth of any sort has proved elusive, but, more significantly for my argument, growth is currently associated with a widening disparity of incomes that can force people even further apart. Failing both money and sameness, the third and perhaps only possibility lies in the politics of democratic engagement. Neither community nor solidarity will come to us ready-made; both have to be constructed through the active involvement of people trying to sort out their differences themselves. I have no illusions here of people wanting to be active in politics full time: I know I don't want this for myself, and I'm not sure I admire it in others. But in however occasional and patchy a way, modern democracies need to increase and widen that participation in discussion and decision that stretches our sense of alternatives, and requires us to confront those who are different from ourselves. Difference need not, but can, be a tremendous barrier between people, and there are few ways of breaching it other than through democracy itself.

Notes

1 Though this is a caricature, it owes much to Francis Fukuyama's much acclaimed essay on 'The end of history', later expanded to *The End of History and The Last Man* (London: Hamish Hamilton, 1992).
2 Shulamith Firestone, *The Dialectic of Sex* (London: Paladin, 1970).
3 Ann Snitow discusses the making of Firestone into a 'demon text' in her interesting chronology of feminist perspectives on mothering. See her 'Feminism and motherhood: an American reading', *Feminist Review*, 40 (1992).
4 See Heidi Hartmann, 'The unhappy marriage of Marxism and feminism: towards a more progressive union', repr. in L. Sargent (ed.), *Women and Revolution* (London: Pluto, 1981).
5 For one of the last major collections on this issue, see Z. Eisenstein (ed.), *Capitalist Patriarchy and the Case for Socialist Feminism* (New York: Longman, 1979).
6 Michèle Barrett, 'Words and things: materialism and method in contemporary feminist analysis', in *Destabilizing Theory: Contemporary Feminist Essays*, ed. M. Barrett and A. Phillips (Cambridge: Polity; Stanford, CT: Stanford University Press, 1992).
7 I am thinking, for example, of the list that Iris Marion Young suggests as a tentative indication of oppressed groups in contemporary America: 'women, blacks, Native Americans, Chicanos, Puerto Ricans and other Spanish-speaking Americans, Asian Americans, gay men, lesbians, working-class people, poor people, old people, and mentally and physically disabled people'. In 'Polity and group difference: a critique of the ideal of universal citizenship', *Ethics*, 99 (1989), p. 261.
8 In 1992, the Conservative government announced the closure of a further 31 pits, and was astonished by the broad-based and passionate opposition (extending even into the ranks of Conservative back-bench MPs) that this decision provoked. After extensive lobbying and major national demonstrations, the government agreed to a temporary reprieve, though at the time of writing it still seems that these pits will close.
9 G. A. Cohen, *Karl Marx's Theory of History: A Defence* (Princeton, NJ:

Princeton University Press, 1978); John Roemer, *A General Theory of Exploitation and Class* (Cambridge, MA: Harvard University Press, 1982); Jon Elster, *Making Sense of Marx* (Cambridge: Cambridge University Press, 1985).

10 Carole Pateman, *The Sexual Contract* (Cambridge: Polity, 1988).

11 For example, Birte Siim, 'Towards a feminist rethinking of the welfare state', in *The Political Interests of Gender*, ed. K. B. Jones and A. G. Jonsdottir (London: Sage, 1988).

12 Sheldon Wolin, 'What revolutionary action means today', *Democracy*, 2 (1982) p. 27; repr. in C. Mouffe (ed.), *Dimensions of Radical Democracy*, (London: Verso, 1992).

13 Benjamin Barber, *Strong Democracy: Participatory Politics for A New Age* (Berkeley: University of California Press, 1984); Young, 'Polity and group difference'.

14 Rodney Barker, 'Note on Anne Phillips *Engendering Democracy*', *Political Studies*, 39, 4 (1992), p. 795.

15 Giovanni Sartori, *The Theory of Democracy Revisited: Part One: The Contemporary Debate* (London: Chatham House, 1987), p. 114.

16 This issue has emerged as a central concern in the implementation of the 1965 Voting Rights Act in the USA, which began as a set of measures to guarantee black Americans their equal right to register as voters, but subsequently developed to challenge electoral procedures that were denying black Americans the opportunity to elect black representatives. The current emphasis is on creating single-member districts in black majority areas, which can then elect black representatives. But as Lani Guinier points out, this strategy can at best deliver a minority black presence; failing a broader coalition between black and white voters and black and white representatives, there is no guarantee that the needs of black Americans will be addressed in policy decisions. See Lani Guinier, 'The triumph of tokenism: the Voting Rights Act and the theory of black electoral success', *Michigan Law Review*, 89, 5 (1991), pp. 1077–1154.

17 Thomas Byrne Edsall with Mary D. Edsall, *Chain Reaction: The Impact of Race, Rights, and Taxes on American Politics* (New York: Norton, 1991).

18 Thomas Byrne Edsall with Mary D. Edsall, 'Race', *Atlantic Monthly*, (May 1991), p. 54.

19 Jean Leca, 'Questions on citizenship', in *Dimensions of Radical Democracy: Pluralism, Citizenship, Community*, ed. Chantal Mouffe (London: Verso, 1992), p. 30.

1

Fraternity

In the gloom of present-day politics, socialists may well lose themselves in nostalgic dreams of fraternity. We feel ourselves hemmed in by a world of self-interest, and experience the daily weakening of those bonds of class and community which gave the socialist movement so much of its strength. The world we now inhabit seems markedly individualist; we cast around in trepidation for some surviving signs of collective feeling.

We talk forlornly of the old back-to-backs with their bustling street life, compare them wistfully with anonymous tower blocks. We recall the mining communities where workers shared their poverty and danger, then shudder at the new towns with their semi-detacheds and their holidays in Spain. We have, perhaps, fond memories of the extended family where each generation played its role, and we shake our heads at its nuclear substitute with granny condemned to an old people's home. It is a theme extensively developed by Jeremy Seabrook, and the popularity of his writings shows how widely his anxieties are shared.[1] Self-help, self-interest, self-protection – these seem the catchwords of today. Fraternity, solidarity, even co-operation, look sadly out of place.

Socialists do their best to resist nostalgia, but even the strongest will quail before such images. Socialism has always invoked some vision of community and usually frowned on unrestrained individualism. The ideal has been solidarity rather than division, working together rather than alone, collective rather than individual action. Partly this is no more than efficiency: to change the world we need the weight of numbers; to end poverty we need the power of socialized production. But for most of us there is a positive as well as a pragmatic side. The 'social' in socialism has always had at least two senses. Socialists believe in co-ordination, arguing that conscious planning will serve us better than unregulated competition. But we also value the very process of working together, tending to the view that this is a good in itself.

Thus it has long been a complaint against capitalism that it turns what should be social into an individual affair. The mechanics of the market put a barrier between us, leaving little space for co-operation or concern. Builders, to take one example, are paid to build – and whether they erect houses for the homeless or yet another office block is no concern of theirs. Train drivers are employed to run the trains on time – and who or what they carry is nothing to do with them. Capitalism encourages us to keep ourselves to ourselves, to do the job, take the money, then spend it as we will. It does not promote a caring society, and reserves its greatest praise for those who 'go it alone'.

Socialists have challenged such individualism, and this is one of the points at which we diverge from classical liberals. Socialists would never define their objectives solely in terms of liberty and equality: the finest liberty and most scrupulous equality would still be inadequate if they left us isolated and alone. Social ownership, socialized production, even socialized consumption, are regarded as positive goals. A socialist society would be one in which we acknowledged and developed our common concerns; the movement to create such a society would be one of co-operation and solidarity. Hence large units of production have been favoured over smaller ones, and not just because of economies of scale. Communal child care has been favoured over caring for children exclusively at home, and not merely because it means less of a drain on the energies of parents. Mass meetings have been favoured over ballot boxes, and not only because they give greater weight to the opinions of activists! In all these cases there is a powerful belief that more social means better. As a sceptic might put it, socialists prefer to share their cake in a dingy canteen rather than divide it into equal pieces for each to eat at home.

This aspect of the tradition has been attacked as illiberal and oppressive, and socialists themselves differ over how much importance to attach to it. But wherever each of us draws the line – between the public and the private, the social and the individual – there can be no doubt that the tradition as a whole values the social. It is because of this that we experiment with collective living, because of this that we exhibit such a marked propensity for going to meetings. We worry (perhaps more than we should) over our privatizing tendencies. We are inspired (much less often than we would like) by public demonstrations of solidarity.

Every one of us will have some emotional memory of collective action, or some evocative dream of future unity. For many the formative experience was on demonstrations, rallies or picket lines: we remember the confidence we gained from marching with thousands of others; the thrill of counting union banners from every trade and region; the emotion, perhaps, when the Yorkshire miners arrived to take their place in the Grunwick picket line. Socialism draws much of its intensity from such experiences, and the suggestion that these are passing will arouse deep concern.

I share this concern, but I also worry that it can make us uncritical of what went before. Those who mourn the lost community are often on shaky ground, with an over-romantic view of the past and unnecessarily bleak picture of the present. The mining communities were, after all, never typical of working-class existence; the back-to-back terraces contained all the frustrations of poverty as well as the comforts of belonging; on numerous criteria (the proportion of old people in institutions, the number of young people who leave their home town in search of work) communities are now *more* stable and caring than they used to be. And, as far as fraternity itself is concerned, we should surely start with the admission that solidarity is not socialist in all its forms, that there are versions of it that repel as well as ones that attract. When we hear talk of the old boys' network, or the clannishness of the old school tie, we do not thrill to these exhibitions of community spirit. Solidarity can divide as well as unite, and some of what we have lost we should be glad to leave behind.

Fraternity in particular has a richly archaic ring and I want to argue we should leave it that way. Trade unionists, we know, are still brothers and send fraternal greetings, but now that one trade unionist in three is a woman such language has come increasingly under fire. Our ears are now more finely tuned to the tensions of sexual division and, when the longing for unity is expressed in terms of men, it begins to strike a discordant note. However grand the 'brotherhood of man' once sounded, today it is out of date. When we review the problem of solidarity, we should beware of slogans that seek to unite in the name of division.

I want in this essay to reassess the tradition of fraternity, arguing against any simple strategy of rehabilitation. As a model of solidarity it is flawed and partial, celebrating the unity of men and exclusion of women. As a basis for future action it is increasingly anachronistic, ignoring major changes that have occurred in the composition of the labour force. Crucial as the problem of solidarity is for socialists, we must first acknowledge the defects in our previous traditions, then see what alternatives we can develop to put in their place.

When 'liberty, equality, fraternity' was proclaimed in 1789, fraternity was already stamped by an earlier history. Family imagery was a recurrent feature of feudal life, in France as elsewhere in Europe, and, in the centuries before the Revolution, brotherhood was the other side of the more authoritarian patriarchy. Craft masters claimed their authority from their role as 'fathers'; when pressed to explain themselves, kings tended to play the same card. Patriarchy was the dominant model for authority, and fraternity was its (largely uncritical) complement. Trades and professions typically organized themselves into corporations or confraternities; monks were brothers; so too were freemasons, who flourished in eighteenth-century France.

This kind of fraternity had both its positive and negative aspects. When journeymen, for example, formed themselves into illicit brotherhoods, they were in some ways prefiguring the later trade unions; the brotherhoods found jobs for their members, arranged accommodation for the journeymen on their weary trek around the country, and even put pressure on masters who tried to cut wages or worsen conditions. More impressively still, they brought together journeymen from a variety of trades, spanning the closely guarded boundaries of the medieval world. But, against these progressive aspects, they generated an intense division between one brotherhood and another. When journeymen swore loyalty to their fellow 'brothers', they were also swearing hostility to those outside, and rival compagnonnages (brotherhoods) were often at each other's throats.

> The rivalries between the sects were passionate and sometimes deadly. Compagnons made up scores of songs insulting their rivals, and these were sung at all occasions. When compagnons of different sects encountered each other, they staged ambushes, skirmishes, and occasionally pitched battles, and serious injuries and even deaths could result. Sometimes different sects came to control different cities, and sometimes single cities were effectively partitioned between sects. But mutual hatred, suspicion, and the threat of open warfare were always present.[2]

As a model for socialist solidarity, such a hectic fraternity left much to be desired. The unity was premised on exclusion, and it was a unity derived from a womanless world. The life of a journeyman was that of a single man who roamed from town to town in pursuit of his trade. Women could appear in this world in the guise of 'mothers' – and indeed the women who ran the compagnons' boarding houses were usually addressed as such. There was, however, no room for them as sisters. A young woman was no comrade, but rather the prize the journeyman might seek at the end of his travels. Getting a wife was both proof of success (who but a master could afford to marry?) and guarantee of future prosperity (how else would you find the sons to work in your workshop?). But while you were still a journeyman, women were largely out of bounds. Hence the brotherhood functioned as a community for single males; the bond that drew them together was their shared experience as *men*.

When the revolutionaries raised their cry of 'fraternity' they thought to distance themselves from the closed world of feudal France – but traditions have a habit of reasserting themselves. On the face of it, the Revolution pursued a new ideal, one closer to that of Rousseau. Instead of the old complex of brotherhoods and guilds and corporations, there would be a new community where individuals united as citizens, with no subgroupings to deflect their common interest. Particularism and exclusivity were anathema to these revolutionaries; what they wanted was a fraternity of all brothers in a single nation.

This produced its contorted moments. In 1791, for example, the market women of La Halle donated funds from their corporation (or guild) to the national treasury, and they were thanked by the President of the Assembly in the following terms:

> Mesdames:
> It is not one of the lesser benefits of the Constitution to have destroyed the spirit of individual corporations, so as to make of all Frenchmen only a family of brothers closely united by the indissoluble and sacred bond of Fatherland. In consecrating today to the public cause what previously had been only a symbol of union between a few individuals, you give a new proof of (that) patriotism which had distinguished you since the beginning of the Revolution.[3]

Note how the 'spirit of individual corporations' and the 'unions between a few individuals' are now dismissed with scorn. But note too that what replaced these remnants was a fraternity of *men*. With all their determined universalism, the revolutionaries overlooked their sisters:

in this case, not so much overlooked them, but even thanked them for their services to the family of men! Did no one note this oddity? Was no voice raised to suggest that fraternity is far from universal when it defines itself as a brotherhood of man?

On this occasion we can hardly plead historical naivety, since the revolutionaries were indeed informed of the universal implications of brotherhood. In 1794, for example, they were forced to recognize that if all men are brothers it is nonsense for some men to be slaves. In a remarkable moment of revolutionary fervour, the National Convention declared that the aristocracy of skin was as abhorrent as the aristocracy of birth, welcomed three delegates from San Domingo (including one ex-slave), and announced that slavery was henceforth abolished in the French West Indies. Admittedly it had taken the revolutionaries some years to reach this conclusion, and when they did it was with a cynical eye to the chances of mobilizing ex-slaves to defend their territories against Spanish or British invasion. But they did at least draw the necessary implication. If fraternity was to mean anything, it must extend itself to all men.

Women were not slow to make similar points for themselves. Olympe de Gouges was one of those to speak out against racism, arguing that fraternity must challenge the despotism of colour. She also wrote in 1791 a Declaration of the Rights of Woman. Rewriting the constitution to read 'woman' instead of 'man', she pointed out the irony of a declaration which proclaimed the freedom of men and remained silent on the slavery of women. Women, she suggested, should qualify for every duty and every privilege now claimed by the men: they had the 'right to mount the scaffold' and should be allowed the equal right to 'mount the rostrum'. As it was, she argued, the revolution had legitimized inequality. 'Enslaved man' had freed himself, but, 'having become free, he has become unjust to his companion.'[4]

Olympe de Gouges was a minority voice, and her complaints could be discredited as those of an anti-revolutionary. Her declaration took the form of an appeal to the queen (in the much mistaken belief that Marie Antoinette could be persuaded to speak in the name of all women) and in 1793 she was executed as a royalist sympathizer. But there were other women, more vocal in their support of the revolution, who also claimed their rights as women. The exclusively female Society of Revolutionary Republicans made no overt criticism of male bias in the constitution – indeed its members took upon themselves the role of defending this constitution against the backslidings of the new moderates.

But when they agitated in 1793 for women to wear the national cockade, they too were making the point that women must be citizens. The tricolour was the symbol of the Republic and the badge of citizenship; when they insisted that all women be compelled to wear it, the Revolutionary Republican Women were staking their claim for their rights and duties. Admittedly they found few followers in this, and indeed made themselves extremely unpopular among the women of Paris. Female challenges to male fraternity were still few and far between, but the challenge was there – however easily dismissed.

Through the nineteenth century, fraternity continued on its varied career and, with the development of the European labour movements, began to take on a heavily masculine form. The fraternity of the French Revolution was undoubtedly male and exclusive, but compared with later manifestations it was still a pretty feeble affair. Eighteenth-century France hardly lent itself to the vision of an all-embracing unity; society was too complex and divided; even a brotherhood of men seemed a far-fetched idea. Fraternity as subsequently developed by trade unionists was to tell a different story.

Capitalist industry had little time for the finicky distinctions of the feudal world and, as it asserted its dominance, workers found their similarities beginning to outweigh their differences. It was this of course which inspired Marx and Engels to their vision of a united and class conscious proletariat. As they argued in the Communist Manifesto, capitalism seemed to be destroying the previous basis for division and distinction. 'The bourgeoisie, wherever it has got the upper hand, has put an end to all feudal, patriarchal, idyllic relations.' It had broken up the 'old local and national seclusions and self-sufficiency', making 'national one-sidedness and narrow mindedness' ever more impossible. Capitalism, they argued, was fast diminishing all those distinctions of skill, age, gender, nationality, payment, which once so miserably divided us. Out of this melting pot a new solidarity would surely be forged, and it would be based on the common concerns of *class* instead of those of trade or nation or gender.

So what happened? Capitalism fell far short of its early promise and failed to deliver a homogeneous working class. Instead of internationalism we have witnessed strident forms of nationalism; instead of unity between the sexes, a continued – and in some ways intensified – divide; instead of common conditions and wage levels for all, a systematic demarcation between the skilled and unskilled, high paid and low paid, black and white, 'middle class' and 'working class'. The unity that did

develop was considerably narrower than that envisaged by Marx and
Engels, and was concentrated mainly among male manual workers. These
workers did indeed come to see themselves as part of a working class
(and to this extent the Marxist diagnosis has been vindicated). But they
were aided in their imaginative leap by a partial redefinition of 'working
class' as male. Instead of class solidarity we have seen a more mongrel
variant, in which class and brotherhood are subtly elided. Instead of
transcending gender difference, solidarity became almost inextricably
linked with masculinity. Instead of countering the narrow fraternities of
the craft unions, it drew its inspiration from the old brotherhoods of
the manual trades. Workers did come to see themselves as brothers,
not in the abstract phrases of the 'brotherhood of man' but as real, live,
working men. Class unity became the prerogative of male workers.

Of course solidarity as *practised* has never been exclusively male, but
solidarity as *imagined* has taken its images from the trade union brother.
Unlike the earlier journeyman, this brother is not inducted through
complex rituals; there are no elaborate ceremonies to mark his membership of the group. He is nonetheless instantly recognizable – a somewhat
burly fellow, of middle age and determined expression. He is celebrated
in every labour movement poster and recorded in all our histories of
working-class struggle. He is rarely young; he may – if struggling overseas
– be black; he is never a woman.

In contrast to the abstract fraternity of the French Revolution, this
was a brotherhood premised on real similarities, and perhaps because
of this it all the more firmly excluded those who were different. Brothers
could recognize one another across oceans and continents because what
they had in common was greater than what kept them apart. They could
perceive their basic likeness through all the distinctions of trade and
country, but how were they to recognize themselves in the experience
of women? The characteristics associated with fraternity were all derived
from the male model of work – it took place out of the home, in the dirt
and danger of the workshop – or the camaraderie of the pub.

Women workers also get their hands dirty, and the exertions of domestic labour often far exceed those of 'heavy manual work'. But the
conventional images stress other aspects and make it hard for women
to enter the fraternity. Women are thought of primarily as wives and
mothers: their first task is to care for the children; their first responsibilities are to the home. When whey do work at home, they are isolated
from the unifying experience of socialized production – and patronized
for what is seen as their narrower vision. When they go out to work,

they are treated as temporary migrants from their home territory, and still denied the status of real 'workers'. Add to this the fact that women's jobs are so often in services rather than manufacturing, in offices rather than factories, and we can see their double disqualification from the fraternity of working men.

Yet the composition of the British labour force has changed dramatically over the past thirty years, and conventional ideology needs to move fast if it is to catch up.[5] Since the Second World War women workers have been creeping up towards the half-way mark in the official labour force: after decades when they were only 30 per cent, they have moved steadily up to over 40 per cent. On the other side of the picture, manual workers have slid down towards the half-way mark: twenty years ago, two workers in three were in manual jobs, but now this is closer to one in two. The old centres of male employment have been devastated; new sectors employing women have arisen in their wake. All those industries that gave us our picture of the trade union brother – the mines, steel, shipbuilding, the docks – have faced massive retrenchment. The declining industries have been largely industries which used to be male.

By contrast, the main areas of growth have been in sectors that rely heavily on female labour. Whichever growth area we name, in public services or in private, in manufacturing or in commerce, it is almost invariably associated with female employment. Health, education, banking, electronics, computers – whichever we mention the story is the same. In some parts of the country the transformation has occurred at such breakneck speed that it is predicted that women workers will outnumber men by the end of the century. In Wales, most notably, all the major economic trends have been concentrated into one small area and abbreviated time-span.[6] The overwhelmingly male sectors of coal, steel and slate have taken a sustained battering; the decentralization of office work has favoured women workers; the expansion of health and education services has meant more jobs for women; the investment of multinationals has been in those high technology areas that typically employ women. Economic crisis since the mid-1970s has partially disguised the trends, but the underlying pattern is nonetheless clear. The typical worker of the future will not be a burly man blasting away at the coal face; she is much more likely to be a service worker employed in a well-ventilated, dirt-free office.

Of course many of these new women workers work part-time; of course they still have primary responsibility for the children; of course they still depend heavily on male earnings for their survival. None of these depressing features should obscure the basic fact that women are nearly half the labour force, and that our images of solidarity must adapt themselves to this. Yet as long as fraternity remains our model for solidarity, and fraternity continues as the prerogative of men in manual trades, we shall be left with little to say.

In thinking about where to go from here, it is worth noting that neither the addition nor substitution of 'sisters' solves the problem. However we employ it, the metaphor of the family seems to carry its own logic. Positive as it appears to begin with, it ends us up in trouble. Within the women's movement, sisterhood has certainly acted as a powerful emotional bond, bringing to our political lives a warmth and affinity we usually reserve for what is private. It has tried to transcend the other differences between us, but to do this in a way which gives weight to our individual experiences. It has given women a new confidence; challenged the elitism of much of traditional socialist politics; and, as examples such as Greenham Common indicate, released a creativity and vitality often absent from more conventional mixed movements. Yet for many feminists today sisterhood is fraught with tensions; what can be a unifying bond has often dissolved into division and unease.

Like its masculine counterpart, sisterhood appeals to a sense of shared experience and claims a unity which is more than shared ideas. The analogy with the family makes it clear: this is something deeper and more intimate than voting the same way in meetings. As so often, the language of kinship is employed to assert a powerful and emotive bond. But the other side of this is moralism. It is more testing to be a good sister than a sound political ally, and more distressing to fail in affection than to fail in political will. Those outside the movement have often felt excluded by the atmosphere of sisterhood, sensing that there are more criteria for membership than simply being a woman. Those inside have sometimes found themselves locked in bitter dispute. It has proved impossible to sustain a united women's movement, and for the present at least the 'movement' is largely wishful thinking. That women should break up into smaller groupings, each focusing on different issues and campaigns, is not itself a problem; when the enemy is so pervasive it is hopeless to fight on every front at once. But the division of labour has often been more than that, and a difference of emphasis has sometimes been accompanied by accusation and mistrust.

Women do share a common identity as women, but we are also divided by our different situations: middle-class women from working-class women; black women from white women; women with children from those without; heterosexual women from those who are lesbians. Sisterhood suggests that we can forge a deep and lasting bond, so when our differences threaten to prevent this, they can generate the intensity of defeat. The problem perhaps is this: in the early years of a movement we *can* be swept into a single identity – 'black is beautiful', 'sisterhood is powerful' – but once that first wave of self-assertion is over, the cracks will inevitably appear. This may well be the logic of movements, and of itself no cause for concern. The difficulty is that 'sisterhood' does not ease the transition to a more sober recognition of what divides us.

The family metaphor has a lot to do with this. Whether the ideal be sisterhood or brotherhood, the language of siblings imposes its own constraints. It identifies a common heritage, some shared experience that sets us apart from the rest of the world. It draws the boundaries between my family and yours, pulling us inexorably into its ghettoized confines. Sometimes it will remain an empty phrase – as was arguably the case with the fraternity of the French Revolution – but when it does become real it becomes divisive, and often reduces to a minority of those it claimed to unite. So the fraternity of the working class reduced to that of manual men, and the sisterhood of women to that of the 'good sisters'. As long as we play with the model of the family, it is hard to resist these finer discriminations. We may be willing to *co-operate* with those we see as alien, but we will reserve our affection for those of our own kind. Unity premised on family likeness can be a recipe for disaster. It tends to exclude those from a different family background, and subjects those it embraces to the familiar tensions of family life. In contemporary Europe, where heterogeneity is so much a feature of our lives, it is bound to lead us astray.

Yet we had our reasons for turning to such models, and the problem of solidarity remains. We are, I think, right to reject a politics based on self-interest – this is too fragile a foundation for what we want to build. The interests of workers in employment might be met by policies which condemn those without jobs to continued unemployment; the interests of people in one country could conceivably be met by defence policies which threaten those in other countries with nuclear war; the aspirations of some women could perhaps be met by changes which leave the rest of women stuck where they were. Logic may tell us that this is impossible, that in the long run your interests are identical with mine. But logic looks a poor substitute for the emotive bonds of fraternity.

In criticizing the concept, I am not proposing we abandon all it

represents. Like so much in our lives, politics demands a certain ro-
mance, and the harsh logic of self-interest is rarely enough to move us.
There are reasons why we thrill to those moments of unity, and reasons
why we despair when they seem to elude us. But if we hope to build
solidarity on a firm foundation, we have to start from a clear understanding of the differences that divide us. We will never secure alliances
between men and women, black people and white people, white-collar
workers and those in manual trades if we try to deny the conflicts that
rage between us. Unity premised on simple similarity can be powerful
but in the end restrictive – attractive but in the end destructive. We are
not all the same, and the pretence that we are will not help us to change
our world.

It is here that we *can* learn from the women's movement. For those
prepared to listen, the recent wave of feminism has reminded us that
solidarity is not exclusively work-based. Against all the odds, despite
the isolations of motherhood, the female competition ingrained in our
culture, the relative powerlessness of women workers, women have
nevertheless managed to organize. In campaigns and debates on virtually every aspect of our existence, we have shifted our perceptions of
what is possible and what desirable. In the mere fifteen years of the
contemporary women's movement, women have made an extraordinary
mark on our culture. And all this has come from a movement which
lacks the most basic strengths of trade unionism, lacks in particular that
unity of purpose which is created and daily reinforced in the experience
of socialized production.

If I am right in thinking that such work-based unity is beginning to
lose its power, then we have to look to alternative sources of strength
and solidarity. Socialists had good reasons for believing that solidarity
is created at work, but bad reasons for claiming this as the only site of
political strength. If the women's movement has shown anything, it is
that there are other kinds of unity and other forms of power. Think of
the way the women of Greenham Common have transformed the
debate over nuclear weapons, and compare this with the empty slogans
of those who say that 'only workers' power will stop the bomb'. Of
course a few women camped outside an army base will not change
history; of course the women who take such actions are atypical; of
course the majority of women would find it impossible to join them
there. Yet women *have* identified with Greenham Common on a massive
scale – and opinion polls show how radicalizing this experience has
been.

Greenham Common is not a prototype for all future action, any more than was the male bonding of manual workers in the past. The lesson rather is that there are many different ways of working for a better future, many and varied forms of solidarity. We should, I believe, abandon the search for a single model, discard our last dogmas on the typical 'worker'. Capitalism has not created a homogeneous working class, and, for the foreseeable future, is unlikely to do so. What brings us together *may* be similarities in our work lives, but it may equally be similarities in our home lives. Sometimes it will simply be a common commitment to social or economic change, cutting across considerable differences in the way we live and the jobs we do. We should not act as if the only solidarity worth its name is the one that unites through every aspect of our existence. Rather, we should think of socialist unity as a complicated – maybe even painful – construction from many *different* solidarities, some of which will inevitably be in conflict.

The argument I am putting here may seem a negative one, but it can form the basis for more positive steps. The crucial starting point is not to glorify the past. Some of the old traditions were tainted and divisive; some of what we feel we have lost is better left behind. Whatever solidarity we build on for the future must rest on a new foundation – not the false fraternity that constrains us to a family likeness, but that more complex unity that stems from recognizing and facing those conflicts that can divide us.

Notes

1 See J. Seabrook, *What Went Wrong* (London: Gollancz, 1978); J. Seabrook, *Working Class Childhood* (London: Gollancz, 1982).
2 W. Sewell, *Work and Revolution in France* (Cambridge: Cambridge University Press, 1980), p. 54.
3 In D. G. Levy, H. B. Applewhite and M. D. Johnson (eds), *Women in Revolutionary Paris 1789–1795* (Chicago: University of Illinois Press, 1979), p. 86.
4 Ibid., p. 92.
5 See A. Phillips, *Hidden Hands: Women and Economic Policies* (London: Pluto Press, 1983).
6 G. Williams, 'Land of our fathers', *Marxism Today* (August 1982).

2

So What's Wrong with the Individual?

Equality, like democracy, is something we are all supposed to support, yet over which we patently disagree. And, like democracy, it has lent itself to a spectrum of opinion from reluctant convert to enthusiastic advocate, dividing us up into pessimists and optimists, realists and dreamers, doubters and those who know. Positions on equality suggest a continuum: a range that starts with the legal and electoral equalities that are the conventional minimum of the day, and extends through increasingly egalitarian stances until no hierarchy at all is acceptable. Where people place themselves on this continuum may seem like psychological quirks; but it is also claimed to be a matter of the limits of their thought. Certainly generations of socialists and radicals have appealed to consistency as a means of securing their case. The liberal dips a toe in the water and considers that quite enough; radicals warn that logic demands further immersion.

Minimal equality is sometimes said to be self-defeating, for once the principles of equality are admitted, they carry more substance than was the original intent. To take just two recent examples: Zillah Eisenstein argues in *The Radical Future of Liberal Feminism* that liberal feminism is potentially subversive, and that, qualified as it may seem in its defence of 'mere' equal opportunity, it contains within itself the seeds of a more radical feminism;[1] John Baker suggests in *Arguing for Equality* that 'everything that matters about equality of opportunity points to the much more extensive equality of egalitarianism'.[2] In both cases, the moderate goals of equality before the law or equality of opportunity are said to carry with them considerable equality of condition. Equality is a slippery slope, and, once on it, it is hard to get off.

Richard Norman, to take another example, argues that there is a direct continuity between liberal, socialist and feminist traditions, and that the last two can be regarded as more thoroughgoing applications of the first.[3] He is concerned mainly with restoring the importance of 'equality', but, when he defends liberalism as the worthy progenitor of the egalitarian tradition, the argument can be twisted the other way. Liberalism might deserve some credit for identifying the importance of political and legal equality, but this is a backhanded compliment for, having set things off on the right track, it has been overtaken by more energetic traditions. Pushing the arguments about formal equality towards a more substantial conclusion, socialism and Marxism surely come out with a higher grade. Feminism then zooms in to take top prize. Despite decades of socialist self-congratulation, class was not after all the last word in inequality and subordination, for what about all those further inequalities between women and men? Revealing to astonished gaze how much more remains to be done, feminism exposes the limits of previous thought. The scope and concerns of equality are once more (is this the last time?) enlarged.

The development of ideas does not of course follow this enlightened pattern. There may be individuals who have travelled from liberalism through socialism to feminism, and who felt consistency driving them on at every stage on the way, but the traditions will not arrange themselves so neatly. However attractive the notion of a progressive continuum, the history of equality does not translate as a concept that simply widened in scope. Socialists feel they have have shown up the limits of liberalism times without number; liberals live on to tell their tale. Feminists feel they have completed both liberal and socialist projects; they find their arguments first welcomed and then mysteriously mislaid. This is not just the stubborn obstinacy of those who refuse to recognize reason, but testifies to genuine disagreement over what equality should mean. The continuing debate on the role and legacy of liberalism is a partial reflection of this; my comparison between socialist and feminist views on equality therefore begins here.

It is relatively uncontroversial to say that contemporary notions of equality developed out of seventeenth-century liberalism; but this is uncontroversial precisely because 'developed out of' can mean so many different things. Leaving open almost everything that matters, it does not yet tell us whether the basic tenets were incorporated or more radically transformed. The literature on this has tended to identify the individual as the crucial point of departure, and, in exploring the current relationship between socialist and feminist views on equality, I shall broadly follow this lead. To put the questions at their simplest: can socialists do anything with the liberal concept of the individual? Can feminists do anything without it? The main point I want to make is that the respective positions of socialism and feminism have been recently reversed. It used to be socialism that most vigorously challenged individualist versions of equality, while feminism tended towards a more ambivalent stance. In the past decade, however, there has been a marked convergence between socialist and liberal views, which has carried with it a new consensus on the individual and equality; over the same period many feminists have been moving the other way. My concern here is to indicate and substantiate some of these shifts, and then consider their wider implications.

Socialism and the individual

In the development of the liberal tradition, the individual is abstract and deliberately so. The classical liberalism of Thomas Hobbes or John Locke began from the idea that all men are born equal – even when noting in the same breath tremendous variations in ability and strength. The additional layers of social and economic difference that then accumulate around these individuals were said to be theoretically insignificant. Disregarding the contingencies of social existence, early liberals built their theories around the 'essential' individual as he appeared in the state of nature: free, equal, but lonely and in fear for his life. The argument might be supported by a psychology that attributed particular (usually unpleasant) qualities to human nature, but this was not really the point. The key feature is that liberalism distinguished between the abstraction of the individual and the living realities of actual people, between the very basic and formal humanity in terms of which we were said to be equal, and the multiple differences that in practice kept us apart. The distinction between essential and accidental is central to the liberal tradition. It is a commonplace of political commentary to note that liberals say we are or should be equal, but do not think we are or should be the same. To the irritated critic this can seem like a loss of nerve – to go so far and then quickly draw back. But the argument is entirely deliberate. Notwithstanding any social differences of wealth or status, notwithstanding any biological differences of ability or strength, *as citizens* we should be treated the same. Whatever the differences, they do not matter. They should not be allowed to count.

Socialists have long countered that the point is vacuous, and that, while major economic and social 'difference' is left to run its course, it is pious formalism to say we should all be treated the same. Unmasking the false abstractions of the liberal individual, socialists therefore pointed to the class realities through which individuals live their lives. The equal right to vote cannot guarantee an equal distribution of power, for access to political influence is profoundly shaped by the distribution of wealth, while power in the workplace remains securely in employers' hands. The right to equal treatment before the law will not translate into legal equality, for the laws incorporate the privileges of property, while those with money can ensure more favourable terms. Specifically biological difference never attracted much attention from socialists, who tended to argue that inequalities of wealth and power accounted for virtually all the supposedly biological differences of ability, height or strength, and therefore discounted this layer. On that more intransigent difference of sex, they maintained the usual silence. The crux of the argument was that social and economic inequality *does* count, and that as long as 'differences' of property and class exist, political equality remains gesture at most.

The argument that political equality rests on prior social and economic equalities has usually combined with a trenchant critique of liberal individualism that queries its vision of the society we need. Quite apart from their blind refusal to consider economic and social constraints, liberals are said to reduce the dreams of equality to the formalities of equal rights. In doing so they express an impoverished version of human existence, in which individuals are always and inevitably opposed.[4] Egoistic, competitive, self-possessed and self-possessing, the individuals of liberal theory are all too obviously in need of protection, and, given the dour premises, equal protection through equal rights may well be the best they can do. But for generations of socialists, this defensive equality – leave me alone to do what I want and I'll leave you alone in your turn – stemmed from the mean-spirited competitive world of contemporary capitalism, a world in which other individuals do indeed threaten our interests and the state does indeed act to constrain and repress. To conflate the specificities of capitalism with the essentials of nature was to give up on our hopes for the future. Liberals had

translated the grand ideals of equality into the protective obsessions of
equal rights and claims; in the process they had abandoned themselves
to a profound fatalism in which individuals had to be separate, atomistic,
counterposed.

In abbreviated versions, liberalism was then said to be pro-individual
while socialism was pro-society – a summary that did little justice to
either tradition but, once spoken, proved hard to correct. Marxists
referred repeatedly to the *Manifesto* definition of communism as an
association 'in which the free development of each is the condition for
the free development of all', but this bid to represent the free individuals signally failed to convince. As far as the sceptics were concerned,
socialism – most especially in its Marxist versions – was too closely
linked to heavy diatribes against the individualism of the liberal tradition: how could any individual be safe in such hands? And twist and
turn as they subsequently did over the relationship between individual,
individualism and individuality, socialists had difficulty finding the precise
formulation that would cut the last one free. Decades of protestation
later, they seem to have given up the ghost. Half the radical intelligentsia
is now busy decentring the subject: an approach that cuts through old
dichotomies by dropping both individual *and* society in the bin. The other
half is bent on winning the individual over.

Anyone who has been following recent debates will be able to furnish
examples, and I shall only offer some indications of my own. Part of
what I am thinking of is the new emphasis on tensions between equality
and freedom, and the various retracings of socialism as being primarily
about individual liberty, or primarily about democracy.[5] Socialists have
usually contested the way their tradition was characterized as anti-
individual or anti-libertarian, but till recently the standard argument
was that individuality thrives best in the rich soil of social co-operation,
or that freedom becomes possible only when we are equal in power.
Within the Marxist tradition, the idea that there might be a conflict
between social equality and individual freedom was, typically, brushed
aside; or, more precisely, it was at the point at which people acknowledged such a conflict that they stopped identifying with Marxist ideas.
Today the choices are less painful. Socialists feel more able to voice
their suspicions of simple harmony without relinquishing the claim to
be socialists still. Freed from some of the pressures to orthodoxy, many
now express impatience with the verbal tricks and methodological
miracles through which the tradition has resisted complaint.

For example, the commitment to an economic and social revolution once implied disparagement of 'mere' political and legal equalities. I learnt my socialism in an era when liberal democracy was a term of abuse and military dictatorships were considered different only in degree; socialists often played down threats to existing freedoms, noting that under capitalism no one was free. Such an easy squaring of the circle is much less practised today. The rights and freedoms of the individual are now regarded as an eminently suitable socialist concern. At the same time there has been a loss of certainty over what economic equality involves. Most contemporary (European) socialists have lost their confidence in centralized planning; many have fundamentally revised their views on the market; the majority probably converge on a critique of statism which attaches heightened importance to individual freedoms and rights. The pursuit of economic equality is increasingly associated with a powerful – and not even efficient – state, and, as more and more socialists come to make this equation, they fear that they may be giving up on what is unquestionably progressive in the search for what is dubiously so. Liberals have always insisted on the potential conflict between social equality and individual freedom; the difference with many contemporary socialists is increasingly a matter of degree.

In both epistemology and politics, socialist theory now operates within more explicitly individualist perspective, as witnessed in the development of rational-choice Marxism and the growing interest in the language of rights. John Rawls's highly influential *A Theory of Justice* is a classic of the individualist tradition, deriving a qualified defence of equality from the redistributive principles we might all agree on as fair and just if we did not know whether our personal destiny was to be rich or poor.[6] Taking as its starting point an anonymity of individuals with no interconnection, their rationality devoted only to their own concerns, it is a theoretical construct that breaks every rule in the socialist book – and yet has inspired considerable interest among socialist thinkers today. One example of this is the Italian theorist Norberto Bobbio, whose writings on socialism and democracy frequently refer to Rawls.[7]

On the terrain of political economy, Alec Nove's *The Economics of Feasible Socialism* offers a polemical challenge to what he sees as the utopianism of much socialist thought, arguing that, in the belief that there *should* be no conflict between equality, freedom and growth, socialists have simply turned a blind eye to the warning signs from planned economies.[8] Instead of pretending that the experience of Eastern Europe or the Soviet Union is irrelevant (that is, not really socialist after all) Nove argues that we should be trying to draw the lessons from that experience. The main ones for him are the limits of planning, the continued necessity for a market, the perhaps inevitable conflict (in any time-span that will prove significant to us) between equality, efficiency and freedom. In his challenging work on the welfare state in Britain, Julian Le Grand has suggested further lessons from experiences closer to home. Public expenditure on social services has, he argues, proved a profoundly ineffective strategy for securing equality, for it disproportionately favours the middle class, who extract considerably more resources from the educational and health systems than those in greater need. His argument initially favoured a more radical egalitarianism that would directly equalize incomes,[9] but has become more generally associated with voucher systems as a means of equalizing individual claims. In both works there is a noticeable shift from the concerns of the producer to those of the consumer, and, whatever we may make of this politically, it is important to observe its theoretical effect. It was part of the ABC of Marxism that 'the consumer' was abstracted from class division and that, presenting us to ourselves only in our roles as buyers and sellers, it glossed over inequalities in power. Compared with the producer, the consumer is a highly abstract and individuated notion, but it is the consumer who leaps out of socialist writing today.

My examples are somewhat random, but together they substantiate a major shift in socialist thought. In terms of equality, they translate into a new emphasis on creating the conditions under which we can act and relate as free and equal consumers, and indeed I would characterize much current thinking as a kind of glorified equality of opportunity. This sounds more disparaging than it should, for any substantial equalizing of our opportunities – whether in access to health care, education, jobs, income, housing – would be a dramatic improvement in our lives. But the change in direction rearranges the relationship between liberal and socialist thinking, and legitimates an abstraction that socialists once claimed to despise. Socialists initially challenged the liberal distinction between essential man and contingent worker, boss, landlord, tenant, and worked hard to reclothe those naked individuals in their class-differentiated garments. The abstract individual was thought to be both methodological nonsense and political liability, a construct that had encouraged an ahistorical myopia and led into an impoverished egalitarianism that could not fulfil even its limited claims. Times have changed, and the individual with them. In contemporary socialist thinking, the abstract individual is widely accepted as a meaningful theoretical term.

Feminism and the individual

What, meanwhile, of feminism? The relationship between liberalism and feminism has followed a different route, and the image of the latter as extension of the former has a plausibility that many writers will confirm. The liberal language of individual rights and freedoms had tremendous resonance for women, and, for the nineteenth and much of the twentieth century, it was liberalism rather than socialism that seemed to offer them a way through. The link remains at its most apparent in matters of equal rights for, as victims of often overt discrimination, women can still get mileage out of liberal ideals, still have to operate on what socialists traditionally regarded as that limited terrain of formal equality. More fundamentally perhaps, the individualism that lies behind liberal thinking on equality has a powerful appeal. Much of the personal impetus towards a feminist politics is to do with claiming the space to choose who and what you are – not to be defined, contained and dictated by notions of 'woman'. Or, to put it the other way round, the idea that it should not matter who or what you are has been an inspiration to generations of women, as has the associated notion that we should be regarded as individuals, as 'persons', as independent of the contingencies of sex. Liberals abstracted the essential man from the accident of history and biology, and, while the emphasis on 'man' was a bit of a blow, the basic structure seemed to fit. All right, so we are different. These differences should not be allowed to count.

This claim to equality *despite* difference is the point of greatest contact between feminism and liberalism, but, as anyone acquainted with the history of feminism will know, it reflects only one strand. For the more socialist inclined, the idea that a woman's sex should not matter is as vacuous in its way as the notion that an individual's class should not count: both of them patently do. A politics that tries to transcend (read ignore) difference is one that confirms the inequalities that exist, and it is precisely the pretence that sexual difference is irrelevant that has denied to women the chance of equal jobs or equal political involvement. For women to be treated as equals with men they need substantial changes in the sexual division of labour, in the conditions under which children are cared for and houses kept clean; it is only when such socially constructed differences are removed that equality can become a meaningful term. 'Equal but different' is from this point of view a nonsense, and merely serves to legitimate separate spheres.

There is a third strand that fits neither of these positions. Feminism has moved recurrently between the emphasis on equality and the focus on difference: between a politics that points out the irrelevance of sex and insists we should be treated the same, and an alternative that takes sexual difference as its starting point. The tension runs through every issue and campaign – often enough through each individual as well – and some of the most obvious examples arise in relation to equality at work. Men and women *are* different, and while some of these differences are socially constructed (to use the language of the 1970s, a matter of gender rather than sex), and therefore open to change, others are more intractable. Women menstruate, get pregnant, give birth: how much should *these* differences be acknowledged when it comes to their positions at work? Legislation that restricts the employment of women in what are regarded as dangerous trades, or limits the hours they can work, or prevents them from engaging in (certain kinds of) night work, can be seen as an unjustifiable restriction on women's earning power. Feminists in the nineteenth century wryly noted that this so-called protective legislation for women was in effect a protection for men, and that it helped secure and maintain the male monopoly in all of the higher paid trades. If women are to be treated as equals, then such legislation might appear to be wrong. But should women have to gloss over the fact that they get pregnant and bear children when the result can be treatment that is *worse* than the man's? The point is similar to that made by Marx in his 'Critique of the Gotha Programme'. As long as people have different needs or capacities, then the kind of equality that metes out exactly the same to each of us in turn will effectively mean inequality: the abstract measuring rod of equal rights is insensitive to varying need.

Feminists will not warm to the example Marx gave, which was that the needs of a single man are less than those of a man with a wife and children to support, but the general question is clearly related. Why should being equal mean being the same? Alone among the wealthy countries of the world, the USA has no national provision for maternity leave, and the only limited protection offered to pregnant women came with the 1978 Pregnancy Disability Act, which established pregnancy as being like 'any other temporary disability'(!). This extended to pregnant women the protections and benefits that are enjoyed by other workers who are temporarily disabled: employers can no longer refuse to hire a woman because she is pregnant, no longer sack her because she is pregnant, or compel her to take maternity leave; and where the state or the firm has some system of benefits to cover temporary disabilities, then these now apply to pregnant women as well. A limited kind of maternity entitlement has thus sneaked in by the back door, though it so far covers less than 40 per cent of working women. But note that the whole philosophy is one that denies pregnancy as something specific to women: 'equal treatment' here means treating pregnant women no better and no worse than any other disabled worker. Feminists in the USA have divided in their responses to this, some feeling that women's interests are indeed best served by gender-neutral legislation, and others arguing that women need sex-specific laws and protections.[10]

Embedded in this issue is the abstract de-gendered individual. The feminisms that most closely approximate the liberal tradition will welcome this character onto their side, for, if sexual equality is to be equated with equal treatment regardless of sex, it means we should be 'individuals' and not 'women' or 'men'. This version retains its powerful advocates, but the pendulum has substantially shifted from abstract equality towards engendered difference, and androgynous ideals of degendered personhood are by no means so fashionable today.[11] Liberals presented a notion of equality in which differences should not count; socialists tackled this on the terrain of class with the argument that differences should not exist; and neither gives much assistance to feminist debate today. Strategies for sexual equality increasingly emphasize sexual difference as the starting point, arguing that this can be neither discounted nor eliminated.

Equality must instead be theorized to accommodate differences of sex. As Zillah Eisenstein puts it in *The Female Body and the Law*, we must 'pluralize the meaning of difference and reinvent the category of equality'.[12] Discussions of sexual equality have so far silently privileged the male body: when men and women are treated the same, it means women being treated as if they were men; when men and women are treated differently, the man remains the norm, against which the woman is peculiar, lacking, different. This phallocratic discourse has, she argues, pushed women into a corner – or rather into a choice of two equally uncomfortable ones. Feminism has been endlessly locked into an equality/difference dichotomy. These are the only choices on offer and yet neither will do.

Eisenstein argues that instead of *the* difference between male and female we need to recognize the many differences between women, between men, as well as between the two. The pregnant woman is of course different from the never-pregnant man, but she is also different from the non-pregnant woman, and different in many ways from other women who are pregnant. Allowing woman to be subsumed under the category of mother is as bad in its way as claiming she is the 'same' as man; both alternatives reflect the impoverished either/or choice that has so long limited our sense of the options. Equality should not rest on how similar we are, on how closely we approximate the norm. What we need is a 'multiple plurality' in which being different *matters* (this is not the liberal perspective which calls on us to treat difference as simply irrelevant) but no longer weakens our claims on equality.

In such arguments we see not only the emphasis on sexual difference, but another preoccupation of contemporary feminism, which is the challenge to those false unities that have littered the path of previous theory. When the elegant abstractions of 'he' and 'man' gave way to the more clumsy 'he and she', 'women and men', the debate was about more than linguistic usage. (Exactly the same issues were raised over the less overtly sexist 'working class'.) Categories that presumed to deal with both women and men, without even noting if it was more one than the other, necessarily wrote in the experience of one sex as if it automatically embraced the other. A more careful differentiation would establish that sometimes 'men' means men. Very occasionally, it really does mean both women and men, in which case it ought to say so. Most frequently of all, it pretends to mean both women and men when in practice it talks only of the male. It is this last phenomenon that is the most dangerous. A major theme in current feminist writing is that the liberal 'men' once meant exactly that (no women here), but has now shifted into the third, and more devious, camp. The individuals of liberal theory are presented as if they refer indiscriminately to women or men, but have written into them a masculine experience and a masculine norm. Their abstraction cloaks a masculine body.

'The "individual" is a patriarchal category. The individual is masculine and his sexuality is understood accordingly.'[13] '(T)he individual is a man, in a male body.'[14] The argument is partly historical, and in Carole Pateman's *The Sexual Contract* involves a major reassessment of seventeenth-century contract theory as grounded in a prior sexual contract that established new terms for male access to women. I will not here discuss this challenging analysis – and indeed, if her argument were only historical, then liberals might still find some means of escape. Scattering profuse apologies around them, they could promise to clean up their concepts and wash off those masculine taints. But Pateman's argument goes further than that. Identity is not something that floats freely through the abstractions of consciousness; it is embodied in physical form. Liberalism tries to deny this in the way it presents its individual, abstracting not only from the social and economic 'contingencies' that have so rightly preoccupied socialists, but also from the biological 'contingencies' that make up sexual difference. In doing so, liberals have covered up their equation between individual and man.

The abstract character of the liberal individual in liberal contract theory has been criticized from the left ever since Rousseau's initial attack. But because the critiques invariably pass silently over the separation of male reason from female body in the original creation of the civil individual, one of his most notable features has also been silently incorporated by the critics. The 'individual' is disembodied.[15]

The body has to be excluded in order to carry off the trick. Under the supposedly abstract guise of the individual, liberalism wrote in a version of sexual mastery in which individuals were perceived as possessing themselves and wanting and needing to possess others. Carole Pateman's argument builds on C. B. Macpherson's notion of the possessive individual, but she attributes this phenomenon to the demands of patriarchy as much as to the development of the market. Our notions of equality, of fair and just contract, of individuals and how they should relate, are unfortunately extensions of this. Women have tried for centuries to turn this language to their own advantage – demanding, for example, to be treated as individuals and not as women – but when they do so they get caught in an appalling bind. One example Carole Pateman gives relates to recent endeavours by American feminists to construct a 'gender-free' version of the marriage contract, in which two individuals freely and mutually contract – but for what? Given the nature of the 'individual' and the meaning of contract, she argues, this can only mean a contract between two people who own their own bodies and agree to mutual sexual use. Sexual relations then take the form of universal prostitution, marking the political defeat of women as women.

Carole Pateman has long been one of liberalism's most vigorous critics, and has increasingly identified women as the definitive stumbling block for the liberal tradition. Women, she suggests, cannot be incorporated into the liberal regime of individuals and rights and consent, except in the most uncertain and ambiguous of ways.[16] Existing discourses on equality embody sexual difference, and they confirm the primary status of men. And though may feminists have hoped and believed they could dust down and improve the biased old categories, there are really only two ways to go. Either we carry on with the pretence that the individual is abstract and disembodied, in which case we silently accept his masculine shape. Or we abandon the search for a cleaner abstraction, and admit that there are women and men. 'To take embodied identity seriously demands the abandonment of the masculine unitary individual to open up space for two figures; one masculine, one feminine.'[17] Away with the abstract, the de-gendered, the disembodied. Not the individual, but women and men.

So, just as socialists make their tentative moves towards the individual, many feminists have been turning the opposite way. The individual has joined the list of suspect categories, but, instead of the traditional socialist argument that stressed his egoism and lack of social context, we have a new feminist critique which stresses his masculinity and liking for men. Let me note again (for feminist critique of dead and gone thinkers always proves more acceptable than contemporary attack) that the argument is not just historical. It says not only that the individual of political theory *has* embraced a masculine experience, but also that of its very nature it remains bound to only one sex. We cannot escape the body, and wherever we introduce a disembodied, de-gendered abstraction we will be insinuating one or other sex as the norm.

Can we manage without abstraction?

I find much of this argument compelling, and it certainly helps resolve practical dilemmas that arise in the pursuit of sexual equality, where we have been beleaguered by notions of a norm. Categories like 'the individual', 'the citizen', 'the consumer' are indeed extraordinarily abstract, and feminists are right to draw attention to the dangers inherent in their use. When equality is theorized through concepts which simply *presume* we are the same, then it can end up favouring those who most fit, and forcing all others into a singular mould. Last year's socialists (or certainly the Marxists among them) knew this full well in relation to class, which is why they preferred producers to consumers, workers to citizens, classes to individuals, and argued for a historically specific understanding of justice, equality, rights. Feminism has now taken over this mantle and, with its new emphasis on bodily difference, extended the nature and scope of the critique.

What puzzles me is how far the argument should go. The critique of the individual clearly engages with what has become a dominant issue today, which is the space (if any) for universal concepts, and the role left for abstract thought. The bid to universality is much contested these days, and in regendering supposedly universal concepts – the individual, citizen, equality, duty, rights – feminism has contributed its fair share to undermining grandiose claims. Social and political theorists are now required to query their hidden assumptions, and even those of most universalistic bent have bowed their head to this need. Jürgen Habermas, for example, acknowledges the challenge in a recent definition of the philosopher's role:

According to my conception, the philosopher ought to explain the moral point of view, and – as far as possible – justify the claim to universality of this explanation, showing why it does not merely reflect the moral intuitions of the average, male, middle-class member of a modern Western society.[18]

The implication of some contemporary feminist writing is that this simply cannot be done. Or, more precisely (since the point is not that average middle-class men are incapable of thinking beyond themselves), that sexual difference can be neither ignored nor transcended, but has to be built firmly into the theories. We cannot pull out some abstract humanity in relation to which we are equal. When we try to do this we impose a part as a norm.

This is where I start to get edgy. For the last three hundred years, every oppressed group has found a lifeline in the abstractions of the individual and has appealed to these in making its claims to equality. 'No, it doesn't matter if I am a woman not a man; it doesn't matter if my skin is black or yellow or brown; it doesn't matter if I am a Catholic or a Hindu or a Jew.' The liberal distinction between an essential 'man' and contingent person has served us reasonably well, for, while it buried class and sexual difference as irrelevant and boring, it nonetheless gave us standards of impartiality without which equality is hard to conceive. If we go too far in the opposite direction, we end up with something like Richard Rorty's notion of the self as 'a centreless web of historically conditioned beliefs and desires',[19] and, once we get there, how do we ever stand back from our prejudices and predilections to perceive that those who are different are nonetheless deserving of our respect? Generations of feminists quite rightly saw the abstract, disembodied individual as a weapon they could use in their bid for equality, for, without even entering into those tedious debates about the size of women's brains or the nature of maternal instinct, they could insist that they were human too. It may be that equality does not require this philosophical underpinning, just as it does not require a humanist foundation that attributes substantial content to the human essence. But there is a risk in this, and it is one I would prefer not to run. If we were to given up on our notions of abstract humanity, what if anything would take its place?[20]

The most radical response is to say that the abstract ideals of impartial justice are themselves part of a male ethic, and that there is an alternative morality premised on understanding, empathy and care. This is part of what Carol Gilligan argues in *In a Different Voice*, where she suggests that psychologists and philosophers have extrapolated from male practices to erect a hierarchy of morals that puts logic and justice on top. Using studies of women facing both real and hypothetical moral dilemmas, she identifies an alternative ethic of responsibility which is based on contextualizing each person involved in the dilemma, trying to understand their options and then minimize everyone's chances of pain:

> The morality of rights is predicated on equality and centered on the understanding of fairness, while the ethic of responsibility relies on the concept of equity, the recognition of differences in need. While the ethic of rights is a manifestation of equal respect, balancing the claims of other and self, the ethic of responsibility rests on an understanding that gives rise to compassion and care.[21]

Here again is the contrast between (male) abstraction and (female) specificity that is running like wildfire through much contemporary feminist debate, and if the implication is that the latter is superior to the former then I simply do not agree. Compassion cannot substitute for the impartiality of justice and equality, for compassion is potentially limited to those we can understand – and hence those who are most like ourselves. For feminists in particular, this would be a risky road to pursue, and it was precisely the demand for equality *across* seemingly impassable barriers of incomprehension and difference that gave birth to the feminist tradition.

Yet Gilligan need not assert one ethic *over* another (from my reading of her work, she does not) and, in a sympathetic review of her position, Seyla Benhabib argues that in fact we need both.[22] The very notion of impartial justice (the 'male' standpoint of the 'generalized other') implies being able to put oneself in another's shoes and acknowledge his/her entitlement to those rights we have claimed for ourselves. But this makes no sense unless we also take the standpoint of the 'concrete other', for until we know the individual's concrete and specific history we cannot say whether the situation is like or unlike our own. We must, in other words, be both abstract and concrete; to relate this to sexual equality, we need both the abstract impartiality implied in 'the individual' and the concrete specificity that tells us whether individuals are women or men.

This is an important recommendation, but note that it looks remarkably like what juries already do. Equal treatment before the law appeals at one level to the impartial distribution of powers, benefits and punishments regardless of sex, race or class; and jurors are called upon to lay aside those prejudices and sympathies that will attract them to those most like themselves. At the same time, jurors are often given considerable information on the history and background of the accused, and it is seen as part of the process of justice that these unique circumstances should be additionally taken into account. Juries are therefore asked to combine the abstract with the concrete, to blend together the egalitarianism that is supposed to disregard difference with its apparent opposite that focuses precisely on what marks people out. In this sense, our best practices already fit with what Zillah Eisenstein calls for when she says that 'equality must encompass generalization, abstraction and homogeneity as well as individuality, specificity and heterogeneity.'[23]

The point I am making is that feminists – like juries – can criticize the abstractions of 'the individual' without having to throw all such concepts away. There are many contexts in which what matters are indeed the differences between us: the difference between pregnant and not-pregnant; Muslim and Christian; shy and confidently verbose. We have to nuance our understanding of equality to deal with this multiple difference, but the nuances are required precisely because of an underlying notion of the human condition which disregards differences of sex, race, religion or class. This notion may have no substantial content – there is nothing there if you strip away what makes us different or unique – yet, without it, the mass of complicated variations would not even begin to enter the debate. We need both the one and the other.

It is one of the paradoxes of contemporary feminist writing that so much of it identifies false oppositions, dualisms or dichotomies as the characteristics of orthodox, masculine thought,[24] and yet so much of it also reads like straightforward reversals of what previous writers have said. Feminists are of course as fond as anyone of creating a theoretical stir, but, in sharpening up the differences between ourselves and orthodox thought, there is perhaps a tendency to exaggerate the size of the gap. Thus, if men have been abstract, women will be concrete; if men have talked of the individual, women will talk only of real women and men. In some cases, this sharp dichotomy fits well with the writer's intentions, but in others it does not. When Carol Gilligan, for example, is read as establishing the superiority of the female ethic of caring over the male ethic of justice, it is I think a misinterpretation. When Carole Pattmen is interpreted as saying we can no longer use the language of individual rights, her challenge to the orthodoxy is being read in too simple a way. Left to (him)self, 'the individual' may well cut a swathe through our dreams of sexual equality, pushing women into a pattern defined by the male. But this is not to say that we are only women or men.

Richard Norman has approached this from the opposite direction, arguing that feminists have presented the orthodoxy in too simple a way. He suggests that feminist critiques of equality have gone over the top, and that, in (rightly) challenging particular versions of the concept, they have (wrongly) dismissed it from use. Without agreeing with all his characterization of the debate, I will end on a similar note. It has been the great achievement of socialism (in the past) and feminism (in the present) to strip away the layers of special pleading to reveal first the class and then the gender of supposedly universal beings, and to challenge what are false abstractions. The risk associated with current socialist developments is that, in the desire to accommodate the political importance of the individual, socialists may too readily forget what mattered in the critique of abstraction – and too easily attach themselves to a version of equality that will be only partially applied. The risk associated with current feminist writing is that, in the (necessary) critique of gender neutrality, some feminists may give up on any notion of universal humanity, and therefore lose what gives equality its power. The danger may lie more in (mis)readings of feminist argument than in the substantial content of what feminists have to say. But I will just put it on record that abstraction can't be all bad!

Notes

1 Zillah Eisenstein, *The Radical Future of Liberal Feminism* (London: Longman, 1981).

2 John Baker, *Arguing for Equality* (London: Verso, 1987), p. 148.

3 Richard Norman, 'Socialism, feminism and equality', in *Socialism and the Limits of Liberalism*, ed. Peter Osborne (London: Verso; New York, New Left Books, 1991).

4 C. B. Macpherson has probably done most to develop this argument in, for example, *The Political Theory of Possessive Individualism* (Oxford: Clarendon Press, 1963). A more recent critique of liberal individualism is Benjamin Barber's *Strong Democracy: Participatory Politics for a New Age* (Berkeley: University of California Press, 1984).

5 John Keane, *Democracy and Civil Society* (London: Verso, 1988) is a prominent example of the latter.

6 John Rawls, *A Theory of Justice* (Oxford: Oxford University Press, 1971).

7 See Norberto Bobbio, *Which Socialism?* (Cambridge: Polity, 1986); and *The Future of Democracy* (Cambridge: Polity, 1987).

8 Alec Nove, *The Economics of Feasible Socialism* (London: Allen & Unwin, 1983).

9 See Julian Le Grand, *The Strategy for Equality* (London: Allen & Unwin, 1982).

10 For an excellent discussion of these debates, see Zillah Eisenstein, *The Female Body and the Law* (Berkeley: University of California Press, 1989).

11 See, for example, the articles in Anne Phillips (ed.), *Feminism and Equality* (London: Blackwell, 1987); and the discussion in Lynne Segal, *Is The Future Female?* (London: Virago, 1987).

12 Eisenstein, *Female Body*, p. 4.

13 Carole Pateman, *The Sexual Contract* (Cambridge: Polity, 1988), pp. 184–5.

14 Eisenstein, *Female Body*, p. 77.

15 Carole Pateman, 'The Fraternal Social Contract', in *Civil Society and the State*, ed. John Keane (London: Verso, 1988), p. 116.

16 For the development of these ideas over the last decade, see the essays in Carole Pateman, *The Disorder of Women* (Cambridge: Polity, 1989).

17 Pateman, *The Sexual Contract*, p. 224. The argument, as I understand it, is not that the unitary figure is by definition male (in a matriarchy, for example, it might be woman who becomes the privileged figure) but that it can't be both woman and man. Hence, in any conditions that we are likely to experience, it is automatically going to be male.

18 Cited in Richard Rorty, 'Thugs and theorists: a reply to Bernstein', *Political Theory*, 15, 4 (1987), p. 579.

19 Richard Rorty, 'The priority of democracy to philosophy', in *The Virginia Statute of Religious Freedom: Two Hundred Years After*, ed. M. Peterson and K. Vaughan (Cambridge: Cambridge University Press, 1988), p. 270.

20 I am partly convinced by the answer Rorty himself gives to this question, which is that it is literature and not philosophy than can increase our sensitivity to those who are different from ourselves, but I worry that this is too parochial. See Richard Rorty, *Contingency, Irony and Solidarity* (Cambridge: Cambridge University Press, 1989).

21 Carol Gilligan, *In a Different Voice* (Cambridge, MA: Harvard University Press, 1982), pp. 164–5.

22 Seyla Benhabib, 'The generalized and concrete other', in *Feminism as Critigue*, ed. S. Benhabib and D. Cornell (Cambridge: Polity, 1987).

23 Eisenstein, *Female Body*, p. 221.

24 See, for example, Diana Coole, *Women in Political Theory* (Brighton: Wheatsheaf, 1988).

3

Universal Pretensions in Political Thought

Early feminist arguments – dating back considerably before the French Revolution, but much strengthened by the events of 1789 – often conceived political priorities in terms of extending to women those rights and equalities that were being asserted as the birthright of men. Women applied to themselves rules that were originally formulated for a more limited constituency, and insisted on making universal what had started out far more particular. The case frequently rested on notions of a common humanity, some essential self all human beings share regardless of any differences by sex. And the arguments continually contrasted what men and women currently, historically, contingently are with what under different conditions they might hope to become. Feminists looked beyond the specificities of existing culture and society (cultures and societies in which women might well appear the inferiors of men) to a more transcendent rationality and justice.

This approach embraced key elements of Enlightenment thinking. The belief in an essential human equality despite all secondary differences, the scepticism towards prejudice and tradition, the confidence in external standards of rationality and justice against which to measure the world: all these formed an important context for feminist principles and debate. And while in this period – as it seems in every other – feminism contained within itself a double impetus towards both equality *and* difference, what we might call the universal aspirations towards an essentially human equality was always one part of the scene.

This kind of political argument has become increasingly contentious in recent discussion, with the Enlightenment turning into a code-word for everything we ought to distrust. Michel Foucault has taught us to view the essential and rational self as an insidious form of thought-police; Alasdair MacIntyre has trampled heavily over the pretensions of universal rationality, arguing that all notions of morality and reason are grounded in particular historical traditions;[1] Richard Rorty has freed us from the search for philosophical authority only to dump us on the ground of local contingency where anything or nothing goes.[2] In one way or another, most political theorists have had to deal with the critique of transcendent universals, the debate between classical and communitarian liberalism, the tension between Kantian and contextual moralities, the anti-foundationalism of post-modern approaches, the importance of grounding one's theories of justice in the value structures of the surrounding world. In a range of overlapping but not identical discussions, the Enlightenment has been getting itself a pretty bad name.

These moves against transcultural, transhistorical, transcendent rationality have their counterpart in recent feminist debate, for, after so many sightings of the 'man' in humanity, many have come to view such abstractions as beyond redemption and to regard any claims to universality as therefore and inevitably a fraud. Each candidate for universal status has presented itself in sharp contrast to the peculiarities and particularities of local identity, something that delves behind our specificity and difference and can therefore stand in for us all. But the 'individual' turns out again and again to be a male household head, the 'citizen' a man of arms, the 'worker' an assembly line slave. Each gender-neutral abstraction ends up as suspiciously male.

Feminist patience has worn thin, and there has been a significant (if by no means united) movement away from the abstract universals of the Enlightenment tradition and towards a new emphasis on heterogeneity, diversity and difference. Two crucial arguments have featured in this shift. The first is that, in insisting on equality as something we claim *despite* all differences, women have been encouraged to deny aspects of themselves and to conform to some unitary norm; the second is that this norm was never gender-neutral. Thus Carole Pateman has argued, in a variety of influential texts, that 'citizenship has been made in the male image',[3] and that the belated inclusion of women operates very differently from the original inclusion of men. Sexual differentiation was built into the foundations of modern (that is, the seventeenth century onwards) political thought in ways that have lasting consequences for the very categories through which we think our lives.

In *The Sexual Contract*, for example, Pateman notes that we have inherited a version of free contract between individuals as justifying anything these individuals might do. They can dispose of themselves and their bodies as they deem fit and, as long as the contracts they enter into can be shown to be voluntary, there is no legitimate basis for anyone's complaint. Applied to women, this then justifies prostitution, and, in recent cases, the legal enforcement of surrogacy contracts even if the mother later changes her mind. The crucial point for Pateman is that contemporary notions of the individual, and by extension of free contract, express a masculine presumption that treats the body as separable from the self. So while some (mainly North American) feminists have toyed with 'genuinely gender-free contract' as a weapon they might turn to their advantage, this is too much imbued with the assumptions of a masculine world.

> The logic of contract as exhibited in 'surrogate' motherhood shows very starkly how extension of the standing of 'individual' to women can reinforce and transform patriarchy as well as challenge patriarchal institutions. To extend to women the masculine conception of the individual as owner, and the conception of freedom as the capacity to do what you will with your own, is to sweep away any intrinsic relation between the female owner, her body and reproductive capacities. She stands to her property in exactly the same external relation as the male owner stands to his labour power or sperm; there is nothing distinctive about womanhood.[4]

One implication, Pateman argues, is that, when feminists contest previous theories of what is appropriate to women or appropriate to men, they must be wary of the concepts they bring to their aid. Most importantly, they should resist the impulse towards denying that sex matters. Sexual differentiation is already writ large in political theory, in a manner that has so far served men. The solution is not to eliminate all such references, but to recast the story with both sexes on stage. Human identity is sexually differentiated, and exists in a bodily form. Those who seek to deny the body, who deal only in the abstraction of 'the individual' or 'the citizen', who think it should make no difference whether these individuals are women or men, will be writing in one sex alone as their standard. Women can be encompassed on an equality with men only if sexual difference is first of all acknowledged.

In the links that have been forged between feminism and postmodernism, such arguments have been pushed further along, emphasizing not so much sexual difference as the multiple difference*s* that any theory must take on board. Nancy Fraser and Linda Nicholson see feminism as exposing 'the contingent, partial and historically situated character of what has passed in the mainstream for necessary, universal, and ahistorical truths' and as leading us to query the kind of objectivity that resides in a transcendent 'God's eye view'.[5] They go on to argue that we must equally well question the notion of 'a' woman's perspective, 'a' feminist standpoint, or 'a' root cause of women's oppression. If the universalisms of humanity are suspect, so too are the universalisms of gender, or those most dubious essentialisms of 'woman' or 'women'. The tendency towards universality sometimes crops up as unthinking assumption, sometimes as grand aspiration, but in either case it should be firmly resisted.

The arguments overlap with issues that have arisen in mainstream political debate, and my starting point in this paper is to draw attention to these parallels. In particular, I want to comment on the common criticism that both these developments provoke. In each case, the move away from grand theory and towards a more specific, historically grounded, or else gendered, account, has laid itself open to complaints of incipient conservatism. In feminist literature, the danger most recurrently cited is that of losing the theoretical categories (gender, patriarchy, even women) through which we can understand and then challenge the world;[6] the subsidiary critique, which then applies pre-eminently to those who stress sexual rather than multiple differences, is that we may lose the capacity for criticizing current gender relations. In mainstream theory, the emphasis has been more exclusively on the notions of justice or rationality that can give us any critical purchase on the communities within which we live. When people query the universalizing pretensions of previous traditions, do they thereby limit their radical potential and blunt the edge of any critical attack?

I raise this problem without necessarily resolving it: partly because we need more work on exploring the precise degree of overlap between feminist and mainstream developments; partly because of the perennial difficulties in deducing politics from philosophical positions; partly because I want to query the sharpness with which the alternatives get posed. I argue, that is, against a polar opposition between what is abstract, impartial, gender-neutral, and what is specific, relational, engendered; and I suggest that the best in contemporary feminism is already steering a more middle route.

Communitarian and post-modern critics

In the last decade of political theory, there has been a powerful move against 'grand theory', and especially against the kind of abstract theorizing that deduces principles of rights or justice from metaphysical assumptions that have their foundations only in thought. An increasingly preferred alternative is what has been described as the 'communitarian' approach, a perspective that grounds our moral and political beliefs in the experience of specific communities and challenges the false abstractions of 'the' individual. Within this rather broadly defined (and by no means unitary) tradition, attention has shifted from establishing universally applicable standards of morality or justice towards elucidating the principles that are already present within any given society. The result is, to use Michael Walzer's words, 'radically particularist'.[7] Notions of justice are said to exist already as part of a community's shared intuitive beliefs, but they are often hidden or latent, and need to be brought into more direct light. Grounded as they are in historically specific communities, however, they cannot claim any universal relevance or scope. Nor do they need to. Richard Rorty argues, in his *Contingency, irony and solidarity*, that human solidarity does not depend on a quaintly metaphysical notion of 'humanity' or 'human nature'. It develops rather in those widening ripples of sympathy that make it 'more difficult to marginalize people different from ourselves'.[8] People sympathize across difference rather than because of some basic humanity we might like to think we all share.

The parallel between feminist and mainstream developments has been noted,[9] as has the major distinction, which is that only the feminists engage with the specific differences of sex. The comparison is instructive, for, where feminists have employed their critiques of universality to radical effect, the work of mainstream theorists reveals a more conservative side. Think, for example, of Alasdair MacIntyre, who, in his celebration of Aristotle or Aquinas, is hardly the feminist's best friend.[10] His critique of liberalism seems well placed, if anything, to confirm the waverer in her commitment to Enlightenment ideals, for he manages to present the tradition in its most attractive light.

MacIntyre notes that the theorists of the Enlightenment expected reason to displace authority and tradition, and he describes the project of modern liberal, individualist society as 'founding a form of social order in which individuals could emancipate themselves from the contingency and particularity of tradition by appealing to genuinely universal, tradition-independent norms'.[11] This may not appeal to MacIntyre, but it holds obvious attractions for the social critic, who is impatient with the world as it is. Her interest in modernity is likely to be further enhanced by the contrast MacIntyre has drawn between the heroic and the modern age. In heroic society, he argues, people's sense of moral obligation is at one with their place in the social structure: 'for the given rules which assign men their place in the social order and with it their identity also prescribe what they owe and what is owed to them and how they are to be treated and regarded if they fail and how they are to treat and regard others if they fail.'[12] 'The self of the heroic age lacks precisely that characteristic which . . . some modern moral philosophers take to be an essential characteristic of human selfhood: the capacity to detach oneself from any particular standpoint or point of view, to step backwards, as it were, and view and judge that standpoint or point of view from the outside.'[13]

Against this attractive view of modernity, MacIntyre's main defence is that the project cannot and will not succeed. It sets up what is an impossible goal, and it is the failure to achieve what we should never have attempted that then plunged modern theorists into the babble of emotivism and the trading in moral fictions. Through his historical investigation of different traditions of enquiry, MacIntyre claims to have established that our standards of judgement are always and inevitably formed within, and given their meaning by, the particular traditions of which we are part. For those who might think this a recipe for complacency (if we are stuck within our tradition how do we criticize its norms?) his only response is that, in generating its own standards of rational enquiry, each tradition has engaged in self-criticism and revision – and sometimes defeated itself as a result.

Richard Rorty is equally dismissive of the search for universal, tradition-independent norms, though he goes much further than MacIntyre in accepting *no* authority for his most heart-felt beliefs. Neither capital-letter Reason, nor the rationality-of-this-particular-tradition: Rorty is happy to detach his liberalism from any kind of grounding and accept its force as just historically contingent. Liberals have relied too long – and unnecessarily – on a notion of the common humanity that human beings are said to share, and should now feel free to dispense with this prop. There is no more a universal human nature than there is a universal truth or a universal justice. Our beliefs are local and particular and contingent, but this does not mean we are stuck with no progress or change. For Rorty, it is imagination rather than reason that acts to extend our sensibilities and our understanding of others, it is literature rather than philosophy that increases our awareness of what causes people pain. Philosophy has sent us on a fruitless search for the 'something' that is common to us all – and then hardly knows where to turn when faced with extraordinary difference. Literature, by contrast, develops our skills in imaginative identification, helping us 'extend our sense of "we" to people whom we have previously thought of as "they".'[14]

The emphasis on literature is certainly compelling, as is the sensitivity to what is positive and progressive about difference. But, as critics recurrently note, Rorty's imaginative acrobatics in the realms of theory seem to combine with the most commonplace complacencies when he turns to the Western liberal tradition. 'How', as Nancy Fraser asks, 'can such critical metaphilosophical views sit so comfortably with such complacent political attitudes?'[15] As one of those pursuing the links between feminism and post-modernism, Fraser finds Rorty's emphasis on the contingent and historically conditioned character of subjectivities and rationalities very much 'user-friendly' – something that seems 'open to the potentially transformative voices and aspirations of subordinated social groups'.[16] How can this combine with a smug 'bourgeois liberalism' that has so little purchase on feminist concerns?

The question becomes more pressing when we consider which of the strands in contemporary political theory have proved themselves most sensitive to issues of women's inequality. Despite the common ground that has been cleared between feminists and those bunched together under the rubric of communitarians (I do not include Rorty in this designation), the latter have been notable, if anything, for their incomprehension of feminist concerns. None of the leading figures in contemporary political theory has turned his critical eye on the structure of the family,[17] and it has been left to those more wedded to universalizing abstraction to raise the banner of equality between women and men. To give just one example, Will Kymlicka relies extensively on the situation of women when he defends liberalism against its critics, and uses this to make some telling points about the conservatism implicit in the communitarian approach.[18]

Kymlicka readily concedes the absurdities of abstract individualism, pausing only to observe how little foundation there is for believing that liberals ever held such a view. The crucial point for him is not whether we can imagine a self without attachments, but whether it is possible to detach ourselves from *particular* values or practices or goals. Are we so constituted by the traditions of our own society that it is for ever impossible for us to judge of their worth? Are we so constrained by the shared morality of our own period and community that our assertions on what is wrong only mean 'we don't do that sort of thing around here'? What then, he asks, of the Muslim woman in Egypt who says sexual discrimination is wrong? 'She does *not* mean "we don't do that around here". On the contrary, she is saying this precisely because it *is* done around there, and always has been done, and is very firmly embedded in all the myths, symbols, and institutions of their society and history.'[19]

In mainstream political theory, the move away from universal principles and values has thus laid itself open to the charge of incipient conservatism, and this worrying potential provides a backdrop to the discussion of feminist theory. Not that the criticisms that apply to one development necessarily apply to the other: we need much fuller exploration of the level of convergence before we can confidently comment on this. Nor indeed that philosophy and politics always go hand in hand: I have serious doubts as to how far one can deduce a political position from the conditions of a philosophical stance. But, in considering current debates within feminist political theory, it is important to bear these parallels in mind. Those who seek to change the world will always need concepts that can give them a critical distance from the relations within which they live. If this is so, then how much is at risk in moves against abstract individualism, universal values, impartial justice? Is there a danger that such feminisms could lose their necessary distance?

Engendering or degendering theory?

I commented earlier that the shift within feminism away from the abstract universals of the Enlightenment tradition, and towards a new emphasis on difference and differences, was significant but by no means united; and it would be seriously misleading to present 'sexual difference' as if it were the only or even dominant approach. There is substantial agreement that conventional political thought has offered us men in a gender-free guise, and that all the talk of universal rights or citizenship or rules has taken one sex alone as its standard, leaving the other one out in the cold. The starting point for much of this discussion is the distinction between public and private spheres, which, along with the relentless allocation of men to the first and women to the second, was early identified as the crucial underpinning to patriarchal political thought.[20] Feminist excavation in the classical texts showed this as the major sleight of hand that had excluded women from centuries of debate on citizenship, equality, freedom and rights, for, having been subordinated to men in the private sphere, they were then subsumed under men in the public. Women were thus rendered politically invisible. In text after text, the classical theorists equated the 'individual' with the male head of household, and gave him exclusive enjoyment of any subsequent rights or powers.

The question then arises: how to correct for this bias towards men? While some feminists reject the unitary model altogether, others see the task as making the theories consistent with a genuinely gender-free world. Two examples from a recent collection on *Feminist Interpretations and Political Theory*[21] illustrate the range. In a devastating critique of John Rawls's *Theory of Justice*, Susan Moller Okin takes him to task for the kind of substitution one might imagine that only the classical writers would make: talking of individuals, but then presuming they are male household heads.[22] Rawls postulated what he called an 'original position' from which individuals were asked to consider the kind of principles they would consider fair and just, no matter what their own social standing then turned out to be. If people were kept in temporary ignorance of their own class position, of their wealth, intelligence or strength, if they could not then anticipate whether they would end up in the top ten per cent or the bottom, what choices would they make about the best system for distributing social and economic advantage? Okin points out that sex is the notable exception in all the lists of attributes people are required to ignore: sex-blindness continues to rule.

Despite her criticisms, Okin nonetheless defends the 'original position' as a brilliant idea that 'forces one to question and consider traditions, customs, and institutions from all points of view'.[23] This, she argues, could be pushed towards far more radical conclusions, for hidden within its distortions is something that can argue against gender differentiation and become a way of challenging sexual subordination itself. If justice requires us to think outside of our own personal experience and perspective, then justice may not be compatible with a society that so systematically divides the experiences of women and men. A major precondition for a just society may be eliminating the inequalities between women and men.

Okin thus develops Rawls's argument to what she sees as a logical conclusion, and applies it to sexual relations as well. Yet in the same collection of essays, Moira Gatens stresses the problems Mary Wollstonecraft encountered when she tried to do just this to eighteenth-century principles of equality. Wollstonecraft neglected to note 'that these principles were developed and formulated with men as their object'.[24] From Gatens's perspective, there is limited mileage in a paradigm that posits sexual equality only at the price of sexual neutrality – and she regards neutrality more as 'neutering', as trying to wish bodily difference away. In a particularly striking phrase, she describes the liberal paradigm as offering fair and equal treatment only 'to those activities that *simulate* the neutral subject',[25] and thus having little to say on such matters as rape, domestic violence or enforced pregnancy, where it is precisely women's bodies that are involved. In both political and moral theory, Gatens argues, we have to come to terms with bodily specificity.

The contest these examples indicate has been conducted on a number of terrains – including equality, justice, political representation – and in each case one of the main objections to those who emphasize difference is that they have overplayed their hand. If universal values do indeed impose a masculine norm, then this may be admitted as a problem. But is this really the case? Defending the concept of equality as a central component in feminist thought, Richard Norman, for example, argues that there has been too much confusion of 'equality' with 'identity' or 'uniformity', and that being equal never meant all people being regarded as the same.[26] Defending the universal scope of justice, Onora O'Neill likewise argues that feminists have misrepresented justice as 'not merely universal but uniform', and have failed to see how much it already embraces and acknowledges difference.[27] As should become clear, I have considerable sympathy with these points, and do not see the issue as an either/or choice. But the feminist debate on difference has been more nuanced than such criticisms suggest, and it deals with important substantive concerns.

Equality, justice, representation

The first of these refers to an issue that has long been a focus of feminist concern, which is whether women can achieve social and economic equality with men by insisting that sex should not matter. What, for example, should be the principles that inform equality legislation, and particularly any legislation for achieving equality at work? Should women be calling for sex-specific legislation that builds in protections for (say) pregnant women; or should they be opposing discriminatory legislation that makes any difference between women and men? In the United States this dilemma has arisen most recently over the issue of maternity leave; in Britain it has emerged in considering the remnants of nineteenth-century 'protective' legislation; in virtually any history of the nineteenth- and twentieth century women's movements, it comes out in a tension between those who ground their policies in equality and those who ground them in difference.[28]

In *The Female Body and the Law*, Zillah Eisenstein argues that such dilemmas arise because the man is being taken as the norm, from which the woman deviates at her peril.[29] The male has been the reference point in all our phallocratic discourse, and discussions of even sexual equality continue to privilege his body. Women can say they want to be treated the same – but this means being treated as if they were men; or they can demand laws that are specific to their needs – but this means being compensated for their lesser abilities or role. The fact is that the norm is already sexually specific; and Eisenstein argues for a new version of equality that no longer depends on us all being the same. One point she stresses is that we do not resolve the problem by going only for 'the' sexual difference. We should think rather of a plurality of many differences, so that equality becomes compatible with diversity instead of forcing us into the self-same mould. It is not that all men are different from all women ('women get pregnant, men don't') for there are multiple differences between women as well as multiple differences between men. It does not help to define women through their capacity for child-bearing, and the dichotomy of male *or* female can be as destructive as having to fit within a male-defined norm.

The argument suggests a very radical pluralism, in which seemingly endless differences by sex, race, age, class, culture . . . all have to be taken into account. An obvious complaint would be that this emphasis leads us away from being able even to think of equality, for if people are so complex and diverse it seems impossible to conceive of them as in any sense being treated the same. Eisenstein tries to steer a careful middle way, however, between two options, arguing that equality 'must encompass generalization, abstraction and homogeneity as well as individuality, specificity, and heterogeneity'.[30] It is not a matter of ditching all the abstract universals and putting concrete difference in their place.

We cannot do without some notion of what human beings have in common; we can and must do without a unitary standard against which they are all judged.

This seems to me the right approach, though I am left with an uneasy suspicion as to whether it is so radically different from what people already believe. As Onora O'Neill observes, we are all equally liable to taxes but we pay differently according to what we earn: the notion of a unitary standard which is then varied in its applications is not such a novel idea. It may be that the legislative and judicial debates in the USA have been particularly blinkered in applying a unitary norm, and that experience elsewhere (in countries, for example, where the equal right to work is thought perfectly consistent with provision for maternity leave) already indicates a more complex approach.

The second set of debates, around the concept of justice, centres on a contrast between male abstraction and female specificity, and draws much of its sustenance from Carol Gilligan's *In a Different Voice*.[31] From a series of studies that look at the way children and adults respond to both real and hypothetical dilemmas, Gilligan has suggested that men and women have different conceptions of morality. The former, she argues, are typically guided by an ethic of rights that rests on a fair and impartial application of abstract rules, while the latter are guided by what she terms an ethic of responsibility or of care, that tries to enter into each person's dilemma and contextualize differences in need. Much previous work in this area had operated with a developmental hierarchy which treated the ethic of responsibility as a lesser stage, and Gilligan turns this round to argue that these express different notions of what justice is about. Gilligan does not treat the differences as innate (though her work can certainly lend weight to a more essentialist feminism that then accepts such differences as given) nor does she necessarily assert one ethic as superior to the other. The key question, rather, is whether these two ethics are exclusive alternatives, and whether presenting them as such can lead feminism down the road of rejecting justice and impartiality and rights. In a careful analysis of Carol Gilligan's subsequent writings, Owen Flanagan and Kathryn Jackson argue that she 'shifts between the ideas that the two ethics are incompatible alternatives to each other but are both adequate from a normative point of view; that they are complements of one another involved in some tense interplay; and that each is deficient without the other and thus ought to be integrated.'[32] Their own conclusion – which I would support – is that there is neither a logical nor a psychological incompatibility between the orientations of justice and care: that people can and do use both orientations some if not all of the time; and that this is just as well, for the moral life may well require a multiplicity of virtues.

Part of the problem here is one that attends nearly every theoretical innovation: that, in challenging a narrow version from one side, feminists risk simply situating themselves on an opposite of a false divide. This may be far from the intention of the original theorist but, in sharpening up what is distinctive in the new position, it is easy to reproduce an over-simple dichotomy. This, certainly, is what Susan Moller Okin fears when she says that 'much feminist intellectual energy in the 1980s has gone into the claim that "justice" and "rights" are masculinist ways of thinking about morality that feminists should eschew or radically revise, advocating a morality of care.'[33] Her own view, which broadly echoes arguments by Onora O'Neill and Seyla Benhabib,[34] is that the distinction between an ethics of justice and one of care has been overdrawn, and that the best of moral reasoning must drawn on aspects of both.

In the continuing debates over Gilligan's work, feminists have not on the whole argued *against* justice and impartiality, but *for* a more complex and balanced appreciation of the relationship between emotion and abstract reason, as well as between what makes us different and what it is we all share. The development of the argument then reduces some of the novelty of the original ideas, for, in moving towards a less dichotomous presentation of the arguments, feminists are not reversing all previous positions. If feminists take up the high ground of empathy and emotion *versus* abstract and impartial reason, they are I believe wrong. If they situate themselves more firmly in the middle ground – as increasingly it seems that they do – they may be right but not so strikingly original. To link this back to Zillah Eisenstein's arguments on equality, if feminists suggest that we should concentrate on the differences between us *instead* of the things we all share, they risk losing the language for even talking of people as equal. But if they contend (as she does) that equality must encompass homogeneity as well as heterogeneity, what they are saying is not so dramatically new. The power of the arguments then lies in what they reveal as the limitations of previous thought, that exaggerated emphasis on what now emerges as only one part of the whole.

The final area of debate I want to comment on relates to issues of political representation. Feminists have frequently noted the extraordinary under-representation of women within both elected and non-elected elites, and here they come up against a powerful swathe of opinion that says sex should be an irrelevant consideration. At the simplest level, this surfaces in arguments that say we should choose our representatives by the way they reflect our views, and that whether these people are male or female should not figure as a legitimate concern. At a more complex level, it surfaces in what is otherwise a radically democratic view: the idea that citizenship should transcend the privatized and fragmented interests of the dominant corporate world.

Iris Young has argued that radical democrats often uphold the most transcendent of universal views, and that they thereby reveal themselves as being as much untouched by gender as the orthodoxies they set out to demolish.[35] This is at its most apparent when writers appeal to a notion of universal *rather* than particular interests, and argue that politics should be dealing with what are common rather than private concerns. Those who develop such arguments may be primarily concerned to criticize the subservience to private economic interest, but when they present the public realm as the antithesis to the differentiated 'private' world the argument gets extended to all other aspects of the private sphere.[36] Any kind of local affiliation is then seen as a problem, and group interest or identity are thought of as something we should be trying to transcend. When citizens participate in political decisions, they are expected to aim at the kind of impartial general will that will take them beyond their own personal concerns. As Iris Young puts it, they are being called upon to leave their selves behind.

The crucial point she makes is that this celebration of universal against particular values can all too easily serve the interests of dominant groups. 'In a society where some groups are privileged while others are oppressed, insisting that as citizens persons should leave behind their particular affiliations and experiences to adopt a general point of view serves only to reinforce that privilege: for the perspectives and interests of the privileged will tend to dominate this unified public, marginalizing or silencing those of other groups.'[37] It is, that is, the old, old story. Appealing to the grandest principles of abstract rationality and universal concern, political theorists write in men once again.

Major policy implications emerge from such arguments, and, if there is some uncertainty as to how radically the focus on difference transforms existing perspectives on equality or justice, there is no such question mark here. Iris Young has developed detailed proposals for the specific representation of oppressed groups; these share a similar starting point with the more limited – but in some countries, already implemented

– proposals for quota systems as a way of getting more women elected to political assemblies.[38] In both instances, substantial and practical implications flow from treating people as members of variously privileged or oppressed groups and from stressing the things that differentiate them, rather than the abstract humanity or citizenship they might be said to share. But as with issues of equality and justice, the difficult questions turn on how far one would want to go, and in this case what balance one might hope to achieve between the ideals of the universal citizen and the reality of group differentiation. There is something very attractive in the notion of politics as an activity in which we get outside of ourselves, putting our own personal and group interests into a more general perspective. Any alternative approach suggests a battle between vested interests which the larger groups will inevitably win. Note, however, that Iris Young explicitly contests this implication, arguing that her own emphasis on group representation is entirely compatible with, and indeed will enhance, a revitalized public life. Existing interest groups, she argues, tend to press their own interests as forcibly as they can, without any acknowledgement that they need consider others. In contrast to this, her 'heterogeneous public' would be constantly reminding people that social justice means considering the position of each oppressed group, and would thereby encourage them towards those decisions that are the most just. In this sense, it would not become a matter of universal values versus group difference, but of building unity without denying social difference.

The aspiration towards universality

Commenting recently on the debate between liberalism and its communitarian critics, Michael Walzer has suggested that the two strands exist in an almost symbiotic relationship, and that, 'insofar as liberalism tends towards instability and dissociation, it requires periodic communitarian correction'.[39] The one, that is, recurrently calls forth the other, in a cycle that has no victor and can anticipate no ultimate end. Much the same can be said of debates within feminist theory. In one version or another, there has been a perennial see-saw between the universalizing aspirations of equality ('my sex does not matter, for I am human, just like you') and the assertion of sexual difference ('I am a woman, and that does not make me less equal'). This endlessly recycled opposition is currently transposed into the language of universality versus specificity, but the issues remain broadly the same. Each generation of feminism throws up and debates these competing approaches, each side then moderating the other's extremes.

Yet what strikes me in considering the debates on equality, justice or representation is that feminist arguments have been considerably less polarized than critics sometimes suggest. There is of course a great deal of unfinished business between those who view the inadequacies of modern politics in terms of the illegitimate intrusion of gender and those who see sexual neutrality as a fraud; and we can anticipate much fruitful discussion in the continuation of these debates. But even among those feminists who start from the centrality and intransigence of sexual difference, the arguments are no simple reversal of Enlightenment beliefs.

Some of contemporary feminist theory *does* overplay its hand, presenting the orthodoxy as more straightforwardly abstract and universal than is in fact the case. Some does read as an affirmation of sexual differentiation *against* universal concepts or ideals, and, where it does this, I believe it risks losing what has been a powerful weapon against women's subordination or exclusion. But of the writers I have considered in this essay, Carol Gilligan has no need to set the ethic of responsibility *above* the ethic of rights, even if she sometimes seems to be doing just this; Zillah Eisenstein explicitly identifies with a version of equality that embraces both the abstract and the specific, both homogeneity and heterogeneity; and, with all her celebration of heterogeneity and differences, Iris Young nonetheless associates herself with the kind of public life in which groups try to build on an understanding of each other and do not just press their own specific claims. Those feminists who challenge the universalism of traditional political or moral thought do not just fly off in the opposite direction, and they are their most persuasive, not in counterposing the particular to the general, the sexually specific to the universal, but in emphasizing the interplay between the two. This approach, I believe, substantially alters the pattern of political debate. But it does not alter it as much as we might like to suggest – and, if it did so, it would more probably be wrong.

When the orthodox notions of citizenship or equality have incorporated a masculine body, when the very 'individual' of political discourse has been for so long a man, then it is far too risky to carry on uncritically as if these old-style abstractions can express women's highest goals. But as we turn from this towards a greater emphasis on sexual and other kinds of difference, we do not thereby abandon all the universal pretensions of political thought. We can do well enough without an abstract, degendered, 'neutered' individual as the basis for our aspirations and goals. We cannot, however, do without some notion of stretching outside of ourselves, some capacity for self-reflection and self-distance, some imaginative – and, more importantly, some practical – movement towards linking up with those who have seemed different. This remnant of the old pretensions is perhaps best described as an aspiration or an impulse towards universality: a recognition of the partial, and potentially confining, nature of all our different and specific identities; a commitment to challenging and transforming the perspectives from which we have previously viewed the world; a politics of greater generality and alliance.

The mistake of much conventional theory has been to see this process as one of delving behind the insignificant differences of being to come up with some unified core. The problem is better approached from the opposite direction: of being able, partly through comparison with those who are different, to reconceptualize what we had considered our essential characteristics as if they were accidents themselves. We do have to detach ourselves (however imperfectly and temporarily) from the crucial facts of our sex, our religion, our nationality, our class, our beliefs, so as to enter imaginatively into experiences that can seem so different from our own. This is not to say that we have to deny these features, but, important as sexual/bodily identity is, it is never our only or even essential characteristic. What is central in one context is marginal in another – which is what makes it possible for us to change our perspective.

The pretensions towards a universal truth or universal humanity have been rightly criticized, and the work of many recent feminist theorists has revealed how persistently such abstractions confirm the perspectives of a dominant group. The arguments go further, to cast severe doubt over the possibility of any better abstraction, and to warn against the potentially fruitless pursuit of a genuinely degendered universal. What I call the aspiration towards universality nonetheless remains. In the reworking of contemporary political theory and ideals, feminism cannot afford to situate itself *for* difference and *against* universality, for the impulse that takes us beyond our immediate and specific difference is a vital necessity in any radical transformation.

Notes

1 Alasdair MacIntyre, *After Virtue* (London: Duckworth, 1981); *Whose Justice? Whose Rationality?* (Notre Dame, IN: University of Notre Dame Press, 1988).

2 Richard Rorty, *Contingency, irony and solidarity* (Cambridge: Cambridge University Press, 1989).

3 Carole Pateman, *The Disorder of Women* (Cambridge: Polity, 1989), p. 14.

4 Carole Pateman, *The Sexual Contract* (Cambridge: Polity, 1988), p. 216.

5 Nancy Fraser and Linda J. Nicholson, 'Social criticism without philosophy: an encounter between feminism and postmodernism', in *Feminism/ Postmodernism*, ed. Linda J. Nicholson (London: Routledge, 1990), p. 26.

6 See, for example, the essays by Nancy Hartsock, Susan Bordo, Christine di Stefano, in Linda J. Nicolson (ed.), *Feminism/Postmodernism*.

7 Michael Walzer, *Spheres of Justice: A Defense of Pluralism and Equality* (New York: Basic Books, 1983), p. xiv.

8 Rorty, *Contingency, irony and solidarity*, p. xvi.

9 Marilyn Friedman, for example, notes the striking similarity between feminist and communitarian critiques of the abstract individual, but goes on to explore what she sees as more fundamental areas of divergence. 'Feminism and modern friendship: dislocating the community', *Ethics*, 99 (1989).

10 Nor I think a 'postmodernist', as suggested by Sabina Lovibond in her 'Feminism and postmodernism', in *Postmodernism and Society*, ed. Roy Boyne and Ali Rattansi (London: Macmillan, 1990). For a fuller critical discussion, see Susan Moller Okin, *Justice, Gender and the Family* (New York: Basic Books, 1989), ch. 3.

11 MacIntyre, *Whose Justice? Whose Rationality?*, p. 335.

12 MacIntyre, *After Virtue*, p. 116.

13 Ibid., p. 118–19.

14 Rorty, *Contingency, irony and solidarity*, p. 192.

15 Nancy Fraser, *Unruly Practices* (Cambridge: Polity, 1989), p. 5.

16 Ibid., p. 5.

17 See Okin's *Justice, Gender and the Family* for an excellent discussion of this.

18 Will Kymlicka, *Liberalism, Community and Culture* (Oxford: Clarendon Press, 1989). Similar issues are raised by Philip Green in his discussion of Michael Walzer, where he comments that radical particularism might seem less attractive to those who are excluded from the dominant community; and that when it comes to matters of racial and gender inequality, there is a lot of mileage in the old-fashioned universals that stress our right to be treated the same. 'Equality since Rawls: objective philosophers, subjective citizens, and rational choice', *Journal of Politics* (August 1985).

19 Kymlicka, op. cit., p. 66.
20 For example, Jean Bethke Elshtain, *Public Man, Private Woman: Women in Social and Political Thought* (Princeton, NJ: Princeton University Press, 1981); Carole Pateman, 'Feminist critiques of the public/private dichotomy', repr. in Pateman, *The Disorder of Women* (Cambridge: Polity, 1989).
21 Mary Lyndon Shanley and Carole Pateman (eds), *Feminist Interpretations and Political Theory* (Cambridge: Polity, 1991).
22 Susan Moller Okin, 'John Rawls: justice as fairness – for whom?', in *Feminist Interpretations and Political Theory*. This essay is extracted from Okin's *Justice, Gender and the Family*.
23 Ibid., p. 190.
24 Moira Gatens, '"The oppressed state of my sex": Wollstonecraft on reason, feeling and equality', in *Feminist Interpretations and Political Theory*, p. 113.
25 Ibid., p. 127.
26 Richard Norman, 'Socialism, feminism and equality', in *Socialism and the Limits of Liberalism*, ed. Peter Osborne (London: Verso, 1991).
27 Onora O'Neill, 'Friends of difference', *London Review of Books*, 11, 17 (1989).
28 See, for example, Olive Banks, *Faces of Feminism* (London: Martin Robertson, 1981); or, specifically on Britain, Anne Phillips, *Divided Loyalties: Dilemmas of Sex and Class* (London: Virago, 1987).
29 Zillah Eisenstein, *The Female Body and the Law* (Berkeley: University of California Press, 1989).
30 Ibid., p. 221.
31 Carol Gilligan, *In a Different Voice* (Cambridge, MA: Harvard University Press, 1982).
32 Owen Flanagan and Kathryn Jackson, 'Justice, care and gender: the Kohlberg–Gilligan debate revisited', repr. in *Feminism and Political Theory*, ed. Cass R. Sunstein (Chicago: University of Chicago Press, 1990), p. 43.
33 Okin, *Justice, Gender and the Family*, p. 15
34 O'Neill, 'Friends of difference'; Seyla Benhabib, 'The generalized and concrete other', in *Feminism as Critique*, ed. S. Benhabib and D. Cornell (Cambridge: Polity, 1987).
35 Iris Marion Young, 'Polity and group difference: a critique of the idea of universal citizenship', *Ethics*, 99 (1989).
36 One of the arguments developed by Carole Pateman is that political theorists frequently talk of a distinction between public and private when referring to the distinction between political and economic; they rarely notice the further distinction that divides both of these from the other private, household, sphere. See, for example, her introduction to *The Disorder of Women*.

37 Young, 'Polity and group difference', p. 257.
38 For a fuller discussion, see ch. 5.
39 Michael Walzer, 'The communitarian critique of liberalism', *Political Theory*, 18, 1 (1990), p. 21.

4

Citizenship and Feminist Theory

The 1980s brought with them a new interest in citizenship: indeed, in the case of Britain, the citizen even entered momentarily into the phraseology of party political debate. In 1988, the then Home Secretary, Douglas Hurd, gave a speech which celebrated the 'active citizen' as a necessary ingredient in social cohesion, and appealed to a self-help tradition of voluntary service as an alternative to dependence on the state. Sceptics were quick to identify this as a belated recognition that the market cannot meet all our needs, and that the gradual dismantling of welfare services was throwing up more problems than it solved. But few were happy to leave it at that, and the same year brought with it other explorations on the theme of citizenship from writers positioned to the left of the Conservative Party. Most notable among these were David Marquand's *The Unprincipled Society*,[1] and Raymond Plant's *Citizenship, Rights and Socialism*,[2] but there was also a plethora of journalistic discussions. For a brief moment, citizenship 'became the simple panacea' for all social and political ills[3] – or, as Hugo Young put it: 'Something is rotten in the state of Britain, and all the parties know it . . . The buzz-word emerging as the salve for this disease is something called citizenship.'[4]

Beyond the fleeting fashions of party politics, this new interest in citizenship signals an important shift in political debate. It brings together what had come to be regarded as separate concerns, for it restates the centrality of specifically political rights, but does this in a language of activity and participation. One of the messages it sends out is that political rights and freedoms matter: that citizens need guarantees of their civil and political liberties; that governments should be elected and not arbitrarily imposed. None of this may need saying in the aftermath of the 1989 revolutions in Europe, except that it reverses the direction of much previous socialist thought. For a variety of reasons (many of them good) socialists have been wary of attaching undue significance to the political realm, and have stressed the prior importance of economic and social relations. Political equality can accommodate itself all too easily to structural inequalities in the distribution of wealth and power, and yet these systematically undermine any formal equality in rights. The point has become blunted through so much repetition, though to my mind it still keeps its edge. The problem is that socialists then became too dismissive of the 'merely' political, tending to blur the distinctions between democracy and dictatorship until the difference virtually disappeared. The new emphasis on citizenship is a deliberate corrective to this.

But citizenship does more, for it also expresses growing frustration with the fragmentation and passivities of contemporary life. In the contrast it implies between citizen and subject, it calls for more active participation, more substantial 'citizen' involvement and control. As is frequently noted, this is meant to span responsibilities as well as rights, and it inspires memories of the Athenian citizens rotating their democratic duties, or Rousseau's virtuous men who never missed a general assembly. In the debased version momentarily favoured in official circles, the emphasis was almost exclusively on activities in the social rather than political realm, conjuring up images of the busy-body who keeps the neighbours in line, or does the work of welfare agencies for free. But implicitly, at least, the notion of the citizen refers us back to a rather grander tradition of civic republicanism, which has viewed political activity as the highest form of happiness and considered it in opposition to 'merely' social concerns.

It is this second aspect of citizenship that I want to focus on here, exploring the problems that then arise in considering the relationship between feminism and the civic republican tradition. This is a tradition that owes much of its twentieth-century inspiration to the work of Hannah Arendt, and it counts among its more recent advocates such theorists as Sheldon Wolin, Hanna Pitkin, Benjamin Barber, Michael Sandel and Derek Heater.[5] In its historical antecedents, at least, civic republicanism has been ominously dismissive of femininity and female concerns, tending to treat the distinction between public and private spheres as sacrosanct, and to presume that women will occupy the latter. In its modern-day variants (more continuously associated with American than British political thought), it draws on these ideas to condemn the emptiness of liberal democracy – and particularly that huckstering politics that deals only in interests or material need. This has generated an impressive critique of pressure group politics and the capitulation to market concerns, and, in its dismissal of interest-led politics, it shares a tiny patch of common ground with themes in contemporary feminist thought.[6] It typically combines this, however, with a vision of citizenship in which people must learn to transcend their own immediate but limited location to address wider and more general concerns. The implied contrast between the general and the particular, the political and the personal, seems to place this in opposition to trends in contemporary feminist thought. As Hanna Pitkin puts it: 'From the political ideals of ancient Athens to their recent revival by Hannah Arendt, republican activism seems to be linked to "manly" heroism and military glory, and to disdain for the household, the private, the personal, and the sensual.'[7] What kind of alliance is possible between this and feminist ideals?

Contemporary feminism has been characterized, if anything, by its distrust of grandiose, over-generalized ideas. It has set itself the task of redefining the political to embrace 'the private, the personal, and the sensual', and, in a growing theoretical literature, has subjected apparently gender-free categories to severe and challenging critique.[8] Starting with humanity, moving on to equality, rights, freedom and democracy, feminists have queried most of the basic concepts of political thinking, arguing that theorists have always built on assumptions about women and men, though not always admitted (even to themselves) what these were. One of the most common tricks of this trade[9] is to smuggle real live men into the seemingly abstract and innocent universals that nourish political thought. The 'individual' or the 'citizen' are obvious candidates here.

The old taunt that used to be thrown at those who talked in terms of citizens is that, outside the sometimes life-or-death situation of those who migrate from one community to another, becoming a citizen may not make much difference to one's life. One disadvantaged group after another fought lengthy battles to be included on the list, only to find that social justice and equality still eluded them. The traditional explanations for this have followed one of two routes. The first (which is heavily indebted to Karl Marx's arguments in *On the Jewish Question*) notes that citizen is fundamentally a political category, and cannot therefore deal with substantial inequalities in the social and economic spheres. The argument is considerably more pointed. Equal citizenship is extended to people *despite* all their differences of birth, education, occupation, gender or race, and it is a slippery slope from saying that these differences should not count, towards saying that they don't even matter. Socialists were quick to spot the disturbing implications for those concerned with class inequalities, while feminists have been equally speedy in noting the implications for gender. There is no procedure that has proved itself so well suited to disguising women's oppression as the division into public and private spheres; and, by directing our attention to specifically political or civil equalities, citizenship helps obscure what goes on in the home. As feminists often remarked in the early years of the women's liberation movement, the equal right to vote barely scratches the surface.

The second approach is perhaps more pertinent to what citizenship subsequently became. Against the background of post-war welfarism, T. H. Marshall reconceptualized citizenship as an evolving complex of civil, political and social rights, and thus gave more real substance to the term.[10] In this later version, citizen no longer signalled a readiness to accept the 'merely' political as enough. The problem now was that the concept of citizen could incorporate (a metaphor that is used with more than casual intent in contemporary feminism) even more characteristics of the dominant groups. In her critique of the patriarchal welfare state, for example, Carole Pateman notes that Marshall wrote in a right to employment as part of his conception of citizenship rights – but did this just at the point when architects of the welfare state were constructing man as breadwinner-worker and woman as dependant-wife.[11] If employment is taken as the mark of citizenship, does this mean women are not yet full members, that their citizenship is still second-class? Similar arguments apply to the citizen responsibility for defending his (*sic*) country, for women are almost universally excluded from conscription, and, even when they sign up voluntarily for the armed forces, they are not expected to join in the fight. Does this indicate that their citizenship is partial and help confirm them in a subordinate role?

Such questions give a new feminist inflection to an older socialist suspicion, and suggest that the citizen is less universal in scope than he likes to pretend. Socialists used to criticize the concept as abstracting from the social realities of capitalist and worker, landlord and tenant, rich and poor. Feminists now stress the way it abstracts from differences between women and men. This is not just a reworking of the same ground, for sexual difference raises particularly tangled questions about the relationship between the social and the biological, and how much of what we call sexual difference is open to future change. Partly because of these issues, feminist theorists are divided over where to go next, and while some look to reformulations that will finally eliminate masculine bias, delivering us concepts that are genuinely gender-free, others reject any kind of grand abstraction, seeing this as inevitably imposing one sex as a norm.

The precise delineation of citizenship rights and responsibilities is a problem that deserves our attention but, other than indicating it as an important and unsettled area of debate, I do not propose to pursue it here. My main concern is with the aspect that is even less developed, which is the kind of politics that citizenship implies. Discussion in Britain has perhaps been overly distracted by the non-political citizen espoused by conservative politicians. But whatever its starting point, the language of citizenship refers us back to the traditions of civic republicanism associated with Rousseau or the Greek city states, and forward to a revitalized politics that transcends the self-interest and parochialism of today. This tradition reclaims the centrality of the specifically political. The division between public and private is reaffirmed, with all the attention directed to the former.

This emphasis is not only at odds with many of the themes in feminist theory, but with what was the dominant radicalism of preceding decades. The last surge of interest in a more active democracy took place in the 1960s and 1970s, when "participatory democracies" ... appeared everywhere like fragile bubbles."[12] In these heady days – which wit-nessed the emergence of the women's liberation movement, but also a renewed impetus towards the democratization of the workplace – the gulf between half-hearted and serious democrats was thought to overlap with the division between those who stressed the political and those who stressed the social or economic spheres. Democracy was felt to be impoverished and ineffective precisely because it had been restricted to the purely political realm: it dealt only in the elections of governments and not in the substance of popular control. If democracy was to mean more than the four-yearly foray into the polling station, it had to be extended and applied elsewhere. Those who campaigned for a more active and participatory democracy thus redrew the boundaries of what counted as 'political', identifying the hierarchy and authoritarianism of the workplace and, in the case of the women's movement, the most intimate textures and relations of personal life.

Feminists have pointed to the division that then developed between those who thought primarily in terms of workplace democracy and those who looked to the more sweeping 'democratization of everyday life'; and Carole Pateman has stressed how very orthodox most proponents of participatory democracy remained in 'forgetting' the domestic realm.[13] But whether the emphasis was exclusively on the workplace or on a fuller and more radical spectrum that spanned both class and patriarchal power, both sides seemed to agree on one thing. The route to a more active and enabling democracy lay outside the conventionally political sphere. Sheila Rowbotham has argued that a crucial component in women's movement politics is the importance it attaches to democratic control of every aspect of daily existence, thereby 'widening the definitions of democracy to include domestic inequality, identity, control over sexuality, challenge to cultural representation, community control over state welfare and more equal access to public reources';[14] Carole Pateman has asserted that 'democratic ideals and practice have to put into practice in the kitchen, the nursery and the bedroom'.[15] From this perspective, the concerns of democracy must be shaken loose from the national assembly or the local town hall. Relations of dominance and subordination do not confine themselves to the conventionally 'public' sphere, and the tasks of democracy extend into every corner of human life.

The emphasis on citizenship potentially reverses this trend, for it reinstates the 'political' and looks to this for our greater fulfilment. Participation 1970s-style dealt largely with what its critics considered the micro-level: the housing estate, the university, the local nursery, the community centre, the place of work. Radical politics centred more on movements than on political parties, and what defined these movements was often group identities of gender, race, sexuality or nationality. There was a growing commitment to a politics based around difference, as in the development of autonomous movements around race or gender, the increased importance attached to women's caucuses inside trade unions or political parties, or the emphasis placed on procedures for balancing ethnic or gender representation. With the decline of a traditionally class-based politics, there was more recognition of the claims of different social groups, and more confident self-organization around specific, group-based needs. The politics of the women's movement is only one indication of this.

Citizenship 1990s-style points in a new direction, and, in their preliminary exploration of 'Citizens and citizenship', Stuart Hall and David Held rightly note that difference is 'the joker in the citizenship pack'.[16] If citizen implies a contrast with subject, it also implies a contrast with all the more differentiated descriptions of capitalist/worker, male/ female, black/white, for it accentuates the rights and responsibilities that we share. It is a concept that deliberately abstracts from those things that are particular and specific, and seems to lift us onto a higher terrain. Differences between one group and another then appear more negatively as problems, for the task is to ensure that no group is excluded by virtue of its peculiarities and position, and that equal citizenship is extended to all. More strongly even than this, citizenship often propels us towards an ideal of transcendence, a greater collectivity in which we get beyond our local identities and concerns. When we are called upon to act *as citizens*, we are by implication not acting simply as women or men, black or white, manual worker or professional, home-owner or council tenant; and, however powerful the affiliations that bind us to a particular social definition, we are supposed to be thinking in more general terms. How, if at all, does this relate to the earlier emphasis on different social movements?

British socialists have been somewhat schizophrenic on this issue, and, if discussions of citizenship help clarify the muddle, this will itself be a major advance. Consider the politics of the last fifteen years. Much political rhetoric was expended in stigmatizing those who are out only for themselves, and, while conservatives usually exempted entrepreneurs and the self-employed, socialists made fewer exceptions. Both sides seemed to unite in condemning trade unionists for their narrowly selfish concerns. Those lucky enough to work in the private sector were attacked for pursuing their own wage claims regardless of the requirements of the economy (this was the main conservative argument); from a more radical perspective, they were criticized for ignoring the interests of lower paid-workers, of women, the unemployed or retired. Those in public sector employment were frequently criticized for setting their own conditions as workers above the needs of the clients they should serve. In an age hardly characterized by altruism or generous deeds, 'sectional interest' nonetheless became a term of condemnation or contempt, meaning exclusive concentration on the narrow interests of your own little group.

At the same time, as I have noted, many socialists were moving towards a politics based on group identity, while feminists were arguing the importance of organizing around one's own needs and concerns. Group identity seemed to be good, while group interest was bad – or did it depend on which kind of group? What exactly was the dividing line between pressing one's own selfish and sectional interest and organizing around your needs as a disadvantaged or oppressed group? Was it positive or negative to be partial? Should politics begin from where you are, or start with wider concerns?

Feminism and republicanism

These issues have been most directly confronted in debates among North American feminists – and not surprisingly, for it is in the USA that the traditions of civic republicanism have retained a firmer hold. Mary Dietz is a particularly significant figure here, battling (it might seem against all odds!) to develop a feminist version of civic republicanism and to present Hannah Arendt as peculiarly relevant to feminist ideals.[17] Her starting point, however, is not so much the determined localism of so much feminist thinking on democracy as the rather different 'pro-family' feminism that is represented in the United States by Sara Ruddick and Jean Bethke Elshtain.[18] Both these writers had turned to women's experience as mothers as an antidote to a male metaphysics, and Elshtain in particular saw mothering as the basis for a new politics of compassion that would reconstruct the political sphere.

Elshtain's critique of liberalism focused on the way that liberalism had recast the boundaries between public and private as determinedly separate spheres, a separation which she viewed as degrading and brutalizing political life. Once the links between politics and the familial were severed, politics could be redefined as the most crass individualism, something that begins and ends 'with mobilization of resources, achieving maximum impacts, calculating prudentially, articulating interest group claims, engaging in reward distribution functions'.[19] The heart then goes out of politics, as all the more caring, compassionate and relational values are abandoned to the 'inferior' private domain. Feminism, from this perspective, speaks for these so-called inferior but in reality higher values, which should serve to chasten the arrogance of public power. The experience of mothering, in particular, generates a more generous and less interest-regarding set of values. Mothers do not put their own interests first, for they can never forget the vulnerability of the human child. Women thus bring to politics a kind of morality and civic virtue that can displace the selfish materialism that dominates today.

While Mary Dietz shares the implicit ideal of citizenship as transcending localized and interest-driven claims, she has no time for the argument that this can be nurtured in the private, familial realm. She sees the loving and protective relationship between mother and child as qualitatively different from the egalitarian relationship that ought to operate between citizens – 'when we look to mothering for a vision of feminist citizenship ... we look in the wrong place'[20] – and she argues that it is only in moving beyond the intimacy of family relations that people learn what citizenship is about. Women who do not venture beyond the family or participate in practices beyond mothering cannot attain an adequate understanding of the way politics determines their lives.'[21] 'To be a good mother is not in itself to have the requisite capacity for citizenship. (Good) mothers may also be (good) citizens, but their being (good) mothers does not make them (good) citizens.'[22] The bond between mother and child is intimate; it is also unequal; and in both aspects stands in clear contrast to the relationship between citizens in a state. Mothers must care for their children because their children are too weak to care for themselves, and this 'condition of attentive love' is a far cry from the mutual respect and shared responsibility that should characterize democratic affairs. In political activity, Dietz argues, 'human beings can collectively and inclusively relate to one another not as strong over weak, fast over slow, master over apprentice, or mother over child, but as equals who render judgements on matters of shared importance, deliberate over issues of common concern, and act in concert with one another.'[23] Politics is in this sense necessarily defined in contrast to private life. Democratic politics exists when we relate to one another as equals, not as the more powerful trying to take care of the weak.

Mary Dietz goes on to argue that 'maternal feminism' is incompatible with democratic citizenship in another significant way: that it tries to develop a feminist notion of citizenship from a position of women's superiority. 'Such a premise would posit as a starting point precisely what a democratic attitude must deny – that one group of citizens' voices is generally better, more deserving of attention, more worthy of emulation, more moral, than another's. A feminist democrat cannot give way to this sort of temptation, lest democracy itself lose its meaning, and citizenship its special name.'[24] The problem here is not just the blow to male confidence in assertions that women are better, but that any such presumption acts against the kind of transformation that Dietz sees as part and parcel of citizenship. In terms that almost sum up the republican ideal, she conceives the power of democracy 'in its capacity to transform the individual as teacher, trader, corporate executive, child, sibling, worker, artist, friend or mother into a special sort of political being, a citizen among other citizens.'[25] Citizenship is about transformation, getting beyond one's immediate sphere.

At first sight, these arguments are in direct contrast to those developed by Iris Marion Young in her critique of the notion of transcendence.[26] Taking issue with recent work by Benjamin Barber,[27] Young draws attention to the problems associated with an ideal of citizenship that calls on people to separate themselves from their own identity or immediate location. This appeal, she suggests, best serves those who enjoy a current monopoly of power. 'In a society where some groups are privileged while others are oppressed, insisting that as citizens persons should leave behind their particular affiliations and experiences to adopt a general point of view serves only to reinforce that privilege; for the perspectives and interests of the privileged will tend to dominate this unified public, marginalizing or silencing those of other groups.'[28] The 'transformation' of people into citizens should not depend on us forgetting our own more specific perspectives or grievances; democracies should, on the contrary, be establishing mechanisms through which oppressed groups are directly represented *as groups*.

The gap between Dietz and Young may be more apparent than real, and perhaps hinges on a distinction between transformation and transcendence. Both of them clearly view citizenship as relying on common membership of a shared community where we acknowledge others as being of equal account; and, for both of them, politics brings us into a very particular kind of relationship through which we address the concerns of those who are different to ourselves. Outside our activity as citizens, we can more legitimately ignore what other groups think. It would be absurd to expect workers to take the perspective of employers when they put forward their annual claim, or women to worry about hurting men's feelings when they organize a movement of their own. In our capacity as citizens, by contrast, we are necessarily reminded of other people's claims, and in this sense are impelled to reconsider our initial positions. The point Iris Young stresses is that this transformation should happen adequately enough if we only engage in an egalitarian politics, have therefore to discuss with others, and reach a decision that seems fair and just. By virtue of this alone, we are obliged to recognize others as citizens and arrive at conclusions that they too can accept. We should not *also* be asked to take a 'general perspective', for this general perspective is an establishment myth.

Both writers then arrive at the absolute centrality of politics. For

Mary Dietz, citizenship means leaving the 'private' world of family or neighbours or work, and becoming involved in more general concerns. For Iris Young, citizenship may mean organizing politically around one's group identity, but then interacting with others in order to decide what policies should apply. They may differ over whether citizenship also involves a particular state of mind, but both see it as taking place in a public arena. Both are millions of miles away from the kind of active citizen who picks up the litter but never gives a thought to the political issues of the day. And, despite Iris Young's emphasis on group identity as being a necessary and legitimate part of citizenship, they are also a long way from those arguments that sought to dissolve distinctions between the public and private.

Stuart Hall and David Held argue that, because the rights of citizens are often rights that people hold *against* the state – guarantees, that is, of certain freedoms and autonomy in social life – citizenship 'therefore combines, in rather unusual ways, the public and the social with the individual aspects of political life'.[29] This is true enough if we concentrate on rights but, from the angle of democratic participation, citizenship returns us emphatically to the political sphere. It is not about 'democratising everyday life', nor about enhancing people's participation in their places of work or study. This is not to say it stands in opposition to these ways of increasing people's control over their lives, but, in so far as they deal only with people's condition as workers, students, tenants, parents and so on, they are not what citizenship is about.

The point I am stressing is that this marks a break with much of the radicalism of previous decades, which tended to side-step the political and concentrate on transforming and democratizing the economic and social spheres. It certainly marks a break with much of what feminists have understood by 'the personal is political', for, instead of reshaping politics to cover any arena in which there are relations of dominance and power, it affirms a division between public and private spheres. Or perhaps not spheres. Iris Young argues elsewhere that there should be certain aspects of our lives that we are entitled to treat as private, but no aspect that we are compelled to treat in this way.[30] For example, we should have the right to keep our sexual lives to ourselves and not be expected to answer public queries about what we do in bed. At the same time, however, we should be free to demonstrate publicly on all sexual issues, and none should be excluded from public discussion as inappropriate or trivial or better suited to a private domain. This retains much of what feminists have meant in stressing the political nature of what used to be dismissed as personal or private concerns. But it does it in the context of a distinction between public and private discussion, and retains a qualitative difference between public and private space. The implication, to give another example, is that we would be acting as citizens if we campaigned in public for men to take a full share in the household tasks; we would not be acting as citizens when we sort out the division of labour inside our own home. In the older language of democratizing everyday life, each of these was equally 'political'. In the new language of citizenship, only the one that takes place in a public arena can seriously contend for the name. Again, the point is not that we should stop arguing about who does the housework, just that citizenship acts on a different terrain.

There are those who will be unhappy with this conclusion, though for myself I find it perfectly acceptable, so long as it is not used to disparage the more private work of transforming personal relations. Being a good citizen is not the same as being a good mother; nor is it the same as being a good feminist; nor is it the same as being a good neighbour. There *is* a kind of jump from the way we relate to people in our more private, and even group, relations to what goes on in political interaction. The women's movement has rightly reduced this gap, arguing, for example, for greater consistency between the ideals people espouse in politics and the way they live out their daily lives; or challenging the sharp dichotomy between universal and particular; or querying the notion that being political means 'forgetting' one's own identity or needs. Even after this narrowing of distinctions, something still remains. Politics is a particular kind of activity, and not to be dissolved into everything else.

Though this signals a new direction, it is not so much at odds with what has been happening in feminism, where the importance of the specifically political is in many ways being reclaimed. There is, for example, renewed interest in what can or cannot be done through the more orthodox channels of public policy and official legislation, and there has been a substantial shift from the anti-statism that characterized much of the earlier years of the women's liberation movement in Britain.[31] A different, but it seems to me related, example is the emerging critique of 'identity politics', with arguments that stress the explicitly political alliances that can be forged through organizing for common objectives, instead of the experience-led identities that arise from shared racial or sexual oppression.[32] With the growing emphasis on politics *per se*, there is more chance of bridging the gap between feminism and the language of citizens.

The preoccupations that underpin much of the current interest in citizenship are therefore ones that I share: we do need to reassert the importance of the specifically political; and we do need to campaign for more active involvement and control. It is still an open question, of course, as to whether these concerns are best approached through the concepts of citizen and citizenship, and, in a period in which feminism is exploring the problems in abstract universals, citizenship may seem a particularly unpromising avenue to pursue. Without careful attention to the ways in which particular identities end up masquerading as universal concerns, 'the citizen' threatens to shut down the awakening recognition of group identity and difference. So while there may be no *necessary* incompatibility between feminism and the language of citizens, a lot of hard work will have to go into ensuring that this is so. If that is the case, it might be better to start the journey from some other point.

I feel at this stage rather like Mary Dietz, who observes in her article on 'Feminism and theories of citizenship' that 'the reader who has followed me thus far is perhaps now wondering whether I have not simply reduced feminist consciousness to democratic consciouness, leaving nothing in this vision of feminist citizenship for feminism itself';[33] and who continues with a rather truncated defence that stresses the importance of participation in women's movement politics. Certainly, from the British context, a language that has been harnessed on the one side to the anti-politics of the active citizen, and on the other to the limited constitutionalism of such groups as Charter 88, does not look particularly encouraging. We will perhaps look back in another ten years' time to this flurry of activity to see it as a peculiar aberration, testifying more to the crisis in previous modes of analysis than any real insights such concepts allow. What nonetheless attracts me to these debates is the tradition of civic republicanism that I have indicated in this essay, and the urgency of political action to which citizenship seems to refer. The new emphasis on our role and aspirations *as citizens* raises important questions about the limits in a 'democratization of everyday life', and helps us to look again at the relationship between the political, economic and social spheres. As Mary Dietz notes in her discussion of Hannah Arendt, 'feminism – at least in its academic guise – needs a calling back to pol'tics'.[34] The value of citizenship lies in the way it restates the importance of political activity. If we can only retain enough critical awareness of the pitfalls, this might yet prove itself as a way of dealing with the politics of an extraordinary time.

Notes

1 David Marquand, *The Unprincipled Society* (London: Cape, 1988).
2 Raymond Plant, *Citizenship, Rights and Socialism*, Fabian Society Tract 531 (1988).
3 Derek Heater, *Citizenship: The Civic Ideal in World History, Politics and Education* (London and New York: Longman, 1990), p. 293. Heater provides a useful overview of the late 1980s debates in pp. 298–304. See also the collection edited by Geoff Andrews, *Citizenship* (London: Lawrence & Wishart, 1990).
4 Hugo Young, 'Citizens! The cure-all rallying cry', *The Guardian* (1 September 1988).
5 See, for example, Hannah Arendt, *The Human Condition* (Chicago: University of Chicago Press, 1958); Sheldon Wolin, *Politics and Vision* (Boston: Little, Brown, 1960); Benjamin Barber, *Strong Democracy: Participatory Politics for a New Age* (Berkeley: University of California Press, 1984); Michael Sandel, 'The procedural republic and the unencumbered self', *Political Theory*, 12, 1 (1984); Derek Heater, *Citizenship: The Civic Ideal in World History, Politics and Education*. For a fuller discussion of these and how they relate to feminist concerns, see Anne Phillips, *Engendering Democracy* (Cambridge: Polity, 1991).
6 See for example, Irene Diamond and Nancy Hartsock, 'Beyond interests in politics: a comment on Virginia Sapiro's "When are interests interesting?"', *American Political Science Review*, 75, 3 (1981); and K. B. Jones and A. G. Jonasdottir (eds), *The Political Interests of Gender* (London: Sage, 1988).
7 Hanna Fenichel Pitkin, *Fortune is a Woman: Gender and Politics in the Thought of Niccolo Machiavelli* (Berkeley: University of California Press, 1984), p. 5.
8 A leading figure in this is Carole Pateman, in *The Sexual Contract* (Cambridge: Polity, 1988) and *The Disorder of Women* (Cambridge: Polity, 1989). See also the essays in Carole Pateman and Elizabeth Gross (eds), *Feminist Challenges: Social and Political Theory* (London: Allen & Unwin, 1986); and Mary Lyndon Shanley and Carole Pateman (eds), *Feminist Interpretations and Political Theory* (Cambridge: Polity, 1991). Specifically on citizenship, see also Ursula Vogel 'Under permanent guardianship: women's condition under modern civil law', in *The Political Interests of Gender*, ed. K. B. Jones and A. G. Jonasdottir.
9 I borrow this phrase from Beverley Thiele, 'Vanishing acts in social and political thought: tricks of the trade' In *Feminist Challenges*, ed. Carole Pateman and Elizabeth Gross.
10 See T. H. Marshall, *Citizenship and Social Class and Other Essays* (Cambridge: Cambridge University Press, 1950).
11 Carole Pateman, 'The patriarchal welfare state', in *The Disorder of Women*.

12 Jane J. Mansbridge, *Beyond Adversary Democracy* (New York: Basic Books, 1980), p. 22.

13 Carole Pateman, 'Feminism and democracy', 1983; repr. in *The Disorder of Women*.

14 Sheila Rowbotham, 'Feminism and democracy', in *New Forms of Democracy*, ed. David Held and Chris Pollitt (London: Sage, 1986), pp. 85–6.

15 Pateman, 'Feminism and democracy', p. 216.

16 Stuart Hall and David Held, 'Citizens and citizenship', in *New Times*, ed. Stuart Hall and Martin Jacques (London: Lawrence & Wishart, 1989), p. 177.

17 See Mary G. Dietz, 'Citizenship with a feminist face: the problem with maternal thinking', *Political Theory*, 13, 1 (1985); 'Context is all: feminism and theories of citizenship', *Daedalus*, 116, 4 (1987); 'On Arendt' in *Feminist Interpretations and Political Theory*, ed. Mary Lyndon Shanley and Carole Pateman.

18 Mary Dietz, 'Citizenship with a feminist face'. The two works she discusses are Sara Ruddick, 'Maternal thinking', *Feminist Studies*, 6 (1980), and Jean Bethke Elshtain, *Public Man, Private Woman: Women in Social and Political Thought* (Princeton, NJ: Princeton University Press, 1981).

19 Elshtain, *Public Man, Private Woman*, p. 246.

20 Dietz, 'Citizenship with a feminist face' p. 13.

21 Ibid., p. 32.

22 Ibid., p. 31.

23 Ibid., p. 28.

24 Dietz, 'Context is all', pp. 17–18.

25 Dietz, 'Citizenship with a feminist face' p. 14.

26 Iris Marion Young, 'Polity and group difference: a critique of the ideal of universal citizenship', *Ethics*, 99 (1989).

27 Benjamin Barber, *Strong Democracy: Participatory Politics for a New Age*.

28 Young, 'Polity and group difference', p. 257.

29 Hall and Held, 'Citizens and citizenship', p. 177.

30 Iris Young, 'Impartiality and the civic public', in *Feminism as Critique*, ed. Seyla Benhabib and Drucilla Cornell (Cambridge: Polity, 1987).

31 A recent collection of essays on Australian feminism discusses tensions between 'grass-roots' and statist feminism. See Sophie Watson (ed.), *Playing the State: Australian Feminist Interventions* (London: Verso, 1990).

32 See, for example, Pratibha Parmar, 'Other kinds of dreams', *Feminist Review*, 31 (1989); or Chandra Talpade Mohanty, 'Feminist encounters: locating the politics of experience', in *Destabilizing Theory: Contemporary Feminist Debates*, ed. Michèle Barrett and Anne Phillips (Cambridge: Polity; Stanford, CT: Stanford University Press, 1992).

33 Dietz, 'Context is all', p. 16.

34 Dietz, 'On Arendt', p. 250.

5

Democracy and Difference

When feminists have challenged the proclaimed gender neutrality of 'malestream' political thought, they have frequently lighted on the abstract individualism of supposedly ungendered citizens as a target for their critique. In Zillah Eisenstein's *The Female Body and the Law*, this provides the starting point for a new theory of equality that no longer relies on us being treated the same; in Carole Pateman's *The Sexual Contract* it underpins a critique of contractual models as necessarily premised on a masculine notion of the body as separable from the self; in Susan Moller Okin's *Justice, Gender and the Family* it is developed into a vision of a genderless society as the precondition for fully just relations.[1]

My concern here is with the further implications for democracy and, more specifically, with the arguments that subsequently open up over group identities and group representation. The feminist challenge to the abstract, degendered individual has combined with the earlier critique of those who took class as the only or only interesting social divide to usher in a new politics based around heterogeneity and difference. Not just 'the' sexual difference: the most innovative of contemporary feminist writing moves beyond a binary opposition between male and female towards a theory of multiple differences. The myth of homogeneity is then seen as sustaining a complex of unequal and oppressive relations; and group identities and group specificities are increasingly regarded as a part of what must be represented or expressed.

The argument shares some common ground with issues long familiar to theorists of democracy, where group affiliation and group organization is frequently presented as a counter-weight to the hierarchy of advantages that otherwise attach to citizens as individuals. In their

Participation and Political Equality, for example, Sidney Verba, Norman Nie and Jae-on Kim suggest that systematic inequalities in individual political influence can be at least partially off-set by the power of organization. In particular, they argue, political equality is fostered by explicit confrontation around class, religion, race or other social cleavages, for, where conflicts of interests become part of the organizational basis of political mobilization, this helps boost the participation of otherwise disadvantaged groups.[2] If we take this line of argument seriously, however, then it makes a case for much stronger conclusions about institutionalizing group representation. Democracy implies equality but, when it is superimposed on an unequal society, it allows some people to count for more than others. Group organization by those less advantaged can in principle equalize the weighting but, given the tendency of those with greater individual resources also to monopolize the group-based resources, things rarely work out this way. If equal weighting is to be desired, and group representation is potentially a means of achieving it, then why not develop formal representation for disadvantaged groups in order to guarantee them a more equal weight?

When the discussion deals solely with class, people have been reluctant to follow it through to any such conclusion, for, while the systematic inequities that class introduces into democratic politics are frequently deplored, they are somehow in the end accepted. The issues become more pointed when they concern groups defined by their ethnicity or gender, these being aspects of ourselves for which we can hardly be held responsible, characteristics we can do nothing about. And yet our democracies are significantly skewed towards the representation of white men, who make up the overwhelming majority of our politicians and who determine what gets on the political agenda. Collective action has only mildly modified this pattern. Should we not call for more formal representation of group identities or group interests in order to counteract the current balance of power?

This is one of the questions that feminism raises for democracy, though I would not want to suggest that it is the only – or even the major – concern. Feminism is associated with a richly textured and layered vision of democracy, in which the precise institutions for political representation have tended to play a subordinate role; feminist theorists have scored many telling points against the abstract individualism of ungendered citizens, but few have derived from this specific recommendations on the difference sexual difference should make.[3] The most fully developed policy recommendation is the call for quota systems to achieve parity between the sexes – in parliaments, political parties, trade unions, corporate structures and so on – which need not (and I will argue should not) rely on any substantial notion of 'representing women'. The case for group representation is as yet implicit in feminist theorizing on democracy, while the notion of group interests has already provoked substantial feminist critique.[4] That said, the feminist emphasis on heterogeneity and differences is beginning to introduce new issues into democratic theory and practice, and I will use this paper to explore some of the problems thus raised.

The starting point is that institutionalizing group representation seems to conflict with what has been the movement of democracy, which is typically away from group privilege and group representation, and towards an ideal of citizenship in which each individual counts equally as one. The French Revolution shattered the principle of representation according to Estates; in all countries that lay claim to the title of democracy, the transition to universal suffrage contested and eliminated the various group definitions – by property, by education, by sex or by race – that had previously organized the distribution of power. Democracy, in this sense, has been viewed as a challenge to special interest groups, and not only because these tend to confirm dominant interests. Many contemporary radicals see the ideals of democracy as pointing towards a politics in which people will transcend their localized and partial concerns, getting beyond the narrow materialism of special interest to address the needs of the community instead. This is the foundation stone, for example, of Benjamin Barber's *Strong Democracy*, where the case for a more active and participatory democracy rests on the transformative powers of democratic discussion and talk. Liberal democracy, he argues, accepts all too readily the notion of pre-given, frozen interests that can only be counted, protected or suppressed. Strong democracy, by contrast, would bring people into direct engagement with other arguments, needs and concerns, and this more active involvement would help thaw out the rigidity of their initial positions. People might still arrive at the meeting with their minds fixed only on themselves or their group, but after fuller exposure to other people's worries will develop a more collective approach.[5]

This version of democracy has obvious attractions when set alongside the damning complacencies of twentieth-century pluralism, which argued that politics was and always would be a matter of competition between interest groups, and that democracy was sufficiently guaranteed by the chance for any group to compete. But it remains open to precisely the charge that is levelled against pluralism: insufficient attention to political equality. When society is ordered in a hierarchical fashion (as is any society we have yet been privileged to meet) then those groups that have been silenced or marginalized or oppressed will look to ways of enhancing their own representation. They will have little time for appeals to them to set aside their own parochial concerns and consider the issues more broadly. Feminists, for example, have had weary dealings with those who claim that the emphasis on sex is divisive, or that it helps rigidify barriers we might all prefer to see removed. Their response has been typical of previously silenced constituencies: the groups that are dominant need their powers stripped away, but others need to amplify their collective voice.

This is the central message in Iris Marion Young's recent critique of Benjamin Barber, and indeed her work serves as the clearest example of a feminist case for group representation. Extending considerably beyond issues of gender, Young calls on democracies to set up procedures that would ensure additional representation for all oppressed groups. The mechanisms she proposes include public funding to enable such groups to meet together and formulate their ideas; the right of such groups to generate their own policy proposals that would then have to be considered by decision-makers; and the granting of veto powers over matters that are most directly that group's concern. (Two examples she suggests of this last are a veto power for women over legislation affecting reproductive rights, and a veto power for Native Americans over the use of reservation lands.) She has many potential groupings in mind, and her suggested list for the United States is somewhat daunting in its implications. It includes 'women, blacks, Native Americans, Chicanos, Puerto Ricans and other Spanish-speaking Americans, Asian Americans, gay men, lesbians, working class people, poor people, old people, and mentally and physically disabled people'.[6]

The argument deals explicitly with equalizing political influence, for it is only oppressed groups that would qualify for this addition to their political weight. The theoretical underpinning, however, is Iris Young's critique of impartiality, which extends beyond the more quantitative aspects of equality to address the conservatism of an undifferentiated norm. We have inherited from the Enlightenment an ideal of universal citizenship, which, however badly practised, claims to deal with us in our essentially 'human' concerns. The vision of democracy that is associated with this claims to treat us as abstract individuals or citizens, regardless of our sex, race or class. More even than this, it calls on us

to treat ourselves and others in the same selfless way. We are allowed
to voice, but are not encouraged to press, our own specific concerns.
Fairness is then conceived as a matter of putting oneself in the other
person's shoes – but, as a number of recent feminist theorists have
noted, there is an unfortunate asymmetry in this. The injunction may
sound positive enough when addressed to those in comfortable positions of power, who do indeed need shaking out of their specific and
narrow concerns. The same injunction can be totally disabling for those
less fortunately placed. When an oppressed group is called upon to put
its own partial needs aside, it is being asked to legitimate its own
oppression.

   Though he approaches the issues from an opposite theoretical direction, Will Kymlicka deals with related questions when he discusses the
relevance of liberalism to culturally plural societies, his main concern
being to justify group rights for any aboriginal community. What he
means by this is 'a stable and geographically distinct historical community with separate language and culture rendered a minority by con-
quest or immigration or the redrawing of political boundaries';[7] as he
describes it, current legislation in Canada and the USA gives such communities a distinct – and in some ways preferential – legal status. Non-
Native Americans, for example, have only restricted mobility, property
or voting rights in the reservation lands of the United States; non-Indian
Canadians are similarly restricted in their access to reservation land. In
the Canadian North, where the inhospitable environment is enough to
discourage permanent settlement by non-Inuit Canadians, the problem
is not so much pressure on the land. But here the extensive development
projects for exploiting natural resources have brought with them large
numbers of transient workers, who at any point in time are likely to
outnumber the original – and permanent – community. Since these
'migrant' workers may stay for as long as seven years, they are able to
vote and thereby influence the allocation of local resources, but they
may as a consequence tailor local provision to their own requirements.
(One of the issues here is whether schoolchildren should be taught in
one of Canada's two official languages: however transient the development workers, they surely have a right to ensure their children are
educated in either French or English, but this may speed the disintegration of Inuit culture and language.) The problem Kymlicka poses is
whether minority groups can therefore insist on special status and group
rights in order to protect their cultural heritage.

   He argues that they can, and, in one of the many irritants to those who seek a close connection between philosophy and politics, he rests his argument on a very different foundation to that suggested in recent feminist debate. While Iris Young employs a critique of impartiality to underpin her case for group representation, Kymlicka appeals to the principle of neutral concern as his basis for what are on the face of it rather similar conclusions. Liberalism, he argues, is best understood in its classically individualist terms of enhancing our choices over the kind of life we should lead, and it is a tradition that encourages self-examination. Liberals believe that people can (and should) detach themselves from whatever traditions or values they have inherited, for 'no particular task is set for us by society, and no particular cultural practice has authority that is beyond individual judgement and possible rejection.'[8] 'Cultural structures', however, provide the essential context within which people become aware of the options open to them and can then intelligently judge their worth. Where a cultural community is threatened with disintegration, this then puts its members at a severe disadvantage – and it is in order to rectify this inequality that these communities require special status or special protection. One possible political implication is given in recent proposals by aboriginal leaders in the Canadian North: for a three to ten year residency qualification before citizens acquire rights to vote or hold public office; for a guaranteed 30 per cent aboriginal representation in regional government; and for veto power over legislation affecting crucial aboriginal interests.[9] This last overlaps directly with one of Iris Young's proposals.

In both cases, the crucial arguments relate to political equality and the distorting consequences of trying to pretend away group difference or affiliation. Political equality is not guaranteed by the equal right to vote, nor gender neutrality by the abstractions of the liberal individual. Abstract individualism imposes a unitary conception of human needs and concerns, and this serves to marginalize those groups who may differ from the dominant norm. The needs of women then appear as a 'special case' (though women make up half the population); ethnic differences are subsumed under 'the problem of ethnic minorities' (as if ethnicity is only a characteristic of minority – deviant – groups); the pauperization of pensioners is treated as just one of many pressure group preoccupations (though most us will eventually be old). The dominance of a norm is so powerful that it obscures the startling fact that most people lie outside its boundaries. As Iris Young indicates, we would like a politics that is more honest than this: 'we must develop participatory democratic theory not on the assumption of an undifferentiated

humanity, but rather on the assumption that there are group differences and that some groups are actually or potentially oppressed or
disadvantaged.'[10]

The case seems overwhelming, and it calls out for some hard thinking
about the institutional changes that would meet such complaints. Precisely what these should be is more difficult to decide, for it comes up
against the worrying problems of group narrowness and group closure.
No one (I imagine) would want to flee the abstractions of an undifferentiated humanity only to end up in its opposite; no one would
favour the kind of politics in which people were elected only to speak
for their own group identity or interests, and never asked to address any
wider concerns. Even setting aside what we would lose in terms of
competing notions of the common good, such a development could
mean shoring up communal boundaries and tensions, which could be as
oppressive as any universal norm. If cultural diversity is positive, there
is no advantage in restricting its range.

It is worth noting that, even in drawing attention to the plurality of
groups and cultures, both Young and Kymlicka express reservations
over what defines a community or group. Young, in particular, is scath-
ing on the authoritarianism implicit in notions of the 'community', which
all too often serve to iron out multiple identities, and impose another
kind of oppressive norm.[11] Kymlicka hovers around similar reservations
when he notes that some aboriginal women's groups have called for an
external review of aboriginal self-government, thereby indicating their
sense of isolation or suppression within the aboriginal community.
Neither theorist warms to the notion of a group identity that is pre-
given or fixed. Young explicitly rejects the idea that group identities are
defined by some essential set of common attributes; she observes that
most people have multiple group identifications, and that groups come
into being and then fade away. Kymlicka deals only with the historically
specific case of aboriginal communities, and he remains agnostic over
how far his arguments could be extended beyond such groups. A close
reading of his argument suggests, however, that he looks forward to a
time when members of the aboriginal community might choose alternatives to their aboriginal identity and abandon their original group.

Both then recognize the problem of closure, the risk that institutionalizing forms of group representation could block further development
and change. But if this *is* a problem – and I think it is – it surely should
be given more weight. What distinguishes these arguments from the
everyday talk of pressure groups is the case they make for institutional

recognition: not just the softer versions of letting groups carry on with their organization and campaigns, but a harder insistence on getting funding and recognition and powers. The more substantial the powers, however, the more it matters that we might get the groups wrong. Do we say, for example, that wherever a group feels itself oppressed or discriminated against, then there is a *prima facie* case for guaranteeing that group some form of representation? Such feelings could after all be misplaced (one rather facile example suggested to me being the men who have been deprived of their hot suppers by the fact that their wives go out to work). And what if the procedures become counter-productive, strengthening rather than weakening a divide? Nigeria, for example, has experimented extensively with quota systems and federal structures in order to balance demands between different ethnic groups, but there is a strong body of opinion that regards this as perpetuating a damaging three-way competition, recurrently reproduced between three major parties. The smaller ethnic groups were seriously disadvantaged in the first constitution; the subsequent proliferation of states only intensified what Richard Joseph describes as 'prebendal politics', an unhealthy jostling for resources, and offices, and power.[12] Where societies are divided between advantaged and disadvantaged groups, it does seem crucial to establish mechanisms that will equalize the balance of power. But such mechanisms can perpetuate the problem, and may not respond readily enough to change.

No one to my knowledge argues for the extreme reversal of current liberal democratic practice that would substitute group representation for the more general representation by political parties. The issue is more one of complementarity, as in Iris Young's suggestions for strengthening the input of groups into the formulations of public policy. But any call for funding or special status draws attention to the difficulties in establishing which groupings are relevant, and this lends weight to a more cautious approach. There is a powerful argument for enhancing procedures for group consultation, and for concentrating these on groups who have been disadvantaged in the current distribution of political influence. There is a much more shaky case for giving such groups definitive power.

The difficulties in defining what are the appropriate groups are compounded by the additional problems of group representation. It is hard to see what counts as 'representing' a group, for there are few mechanisms for establishing what each group wants. We cannot say, for example, that getting more women elected to local or national assemblies therefore

secures the representation of women. Politicians are not elected by
women's constituencies, and apart from canvassing opinion within their
own parties and perhaps consulting their own coterie of friends, they
do not have a basis for claiming to speak 'for women'. One response
could be to create more substantial mechanisms for consultation and
group organization – perhaps along the lines that Iris Young suggests.
But then anything that relies on people going to meetings (a women's
forum, for example) potentially founders on the limited numbers who
are likely to attend. The people who go to meetings are often a pretty
'unrepresentative' bunch!

The problems of accountability combine with the risks of freezing
what are multiple and shifting identities to set severe limits to the notion of group representation, favouring a weaker version of group consultation over the stronger versions that might include veto power. The
same problems do not, however, apply to the case for political quotas,
which can be and should be distinguished. The extraordinary mismatch
between the kind of people who get elected and the gender and ethnic
composition of the population they claim to represent remains as a
serious blot on the practices of democracy. These problems can be tackled without a notion of group representation.

The case for gender quotas has been pursued with particular success
by women active in political parties in the Nordic countries, largely, but
not exclusively, those on the left of the political spectrum. In the course
of the 1970s a number of parties adopted the principle of at least 40
per cent representation of either sex at all levels of elected delegation
within the party itself: the Swedish Liberal and Communist parties in
1972, the Norwegian Liberal Party in 1974 and Socialist Left Party
in 1975, the Danish Socialist People's Party in 1977.[13] In the following
decade there was a push to extend this to the level of female representation in national parliaments, the mechanisms being relatively straightforward in electoral systems that operate a party list system and elect
according to proportional representation. In 1980 parties in both Norway and Sweden proposed legislation that would commit *all* political
parties to a minimum of 40 per cent of either sex on their electoral lists;
failing the success of this bid, various parties introduced the practice
unilaterally.[14] In 1983, for example, the Norwegian Labour Party introduced a 40 per cent quota for candidates in local and national
elections, while among the parties that remained ideologically opposed
to the principle of a quota system there was also substantial movement.
The Norwegian Conservative Party espouses 'competence' rather than

formal quotas, but women nonetheless made up 30 per cent of its national representation by the mid-1980s.

The results have proved rather spectacular. While Britain has only just managed to lift itself above the 5 per cent barrier in its proportion of women MPs, the Nordic countries stand out as a relative haven for women politicians. By 1984 women had taken 15 per cent of the parliamentary seats in Iceland, 26 per cent in Norway and Denmark; 28 per cent in Sweden and 31 per cent in Finland.[15] In 1985 Norway took the world record, very largely as a result of the quota introduced by the Norwegian Labour Party and the fact that Labour then won the general election. Women made up 34.4 per cent of the Storting (the national assembly), held eight out of eighteen cabinet posts, contributed 40.5 per cent of the membership of county councils, and formed 31.1 per cent of the membership of municipal councils.

Though feminists have employed a variety of arguments in pressing the case for political quotas, the crucial one does not – and I believe should not – rest on a notion of group representation. More than anything, it is an argument in terms of political equality. When the composition of decision-making assemblies is so markedly at odds with the gender and ethnic make-up of the society they represent, this is clear evidence that certain voices are being silenced or suppressed. If there were no substantial obstacles in the way of equal participation, then those active in politics would be randomly distributed according to their ethnicity or gender; the fact that the distribution is so far from random therefore alerts us to these obstacles and the necessity for some countervailing force. The argument can be enhanced by all manner of predictions about how the composition of our decision-making assemblies will be enriched by a wider range of opinions and knowledges and concerns. But the argument is not strengthened – if anything it is weakened – by the more substantial notion of 'representing' a new constituency or group. Accountability is always the other side of representation, and, in the absence of procedures for establishing what any group wants or thinks, we cannot usefully talk of their political representation.

The difficulties that bedevil group representation do not therefore affect the case for political quotas – or indeed for whatever alternative mechanisms could help establish political parity. The one point of overlap – and it is a difficult one – is in thinking about how far one should extend the principle of what I shall call 'mirror' rather than political representation: what exactly are the groups that should count? The standard case against quota systems is a *reductio ad absurdum* that pretends the list will go on and on, and, while I would want to resist the dishonesty of those who prefer no change, the objection contains the kernel of a serious concern. If the arguments in favour of ethnicity and gender are so decisive, what justifies us in stopping at these two: surely the same kind of points could be made in terms of religion, of sexuality, of class? In each case the failure to 'reflect' the distribution of characteristics through the population as a whole should alert us to obstacles that are preventing equal participation. In each case there is then an argument for guaranteeing proportional representation. Where exactly are we supposed to draw the line, and what is the basis for any distinction?

The answer at one level is simple: it is politics that defines the pertinent categories, which therefore and quite legitimately change. This is true even in terms of what I am presenting as the more 'permanently' relevant categories, and perhaps helps explain why the case for parity between women and men has so far met with greater success than the parallel case for parity between different ethnic groups.[16] In the case of Britain, for example, the all-embracing concept of 'black' people rapidly dissolved into a distinction between the Asian and Afro-Caribbean communities, and then subsequently into finer distinctions between a wide variety of ethnic groups.[17] What in this context then counts as 'adequate' ethnic representation? Such questions can hardly be answered in isolation from politics and political mobilizations, and any attempt to settle the matter in advance would freeze the relevant categories at a premature moment of discussion and debate. The same argument would apply to any further extensions of mirror representation. Religious affiliation, for example, becomes more or less pertinent depending on the politics of the society in question, and it would be inappropriate to rule it in or out as a matter of abstract principle. I am not entirely happy with this resolution, for, when politics becomes sole arbiter, this edges too close to an abdication of judgement. These are matters that require much closer discussion.

The general conclusions I draw involve a modification – but also a modified defence – of liberal democracy as we know and loathe it. It is indeed dangerous to pretend that who or what we are is irrelevant, to ask people to submerge their group differences in an abstract citizenship, to say that politics should be only a matter of ideas. Such complacency leaves democracy too much at the mercy of existing power relations, which will just reproduce existing patterns of power. More specifically, the composition of political representatives does matter, and we need the kind of institutional changes that will guarantee proportionality – at least by ethnicity and gender. But we should detach the arguments, for example, for more women in politics – for parity between women and men – from the arguments for representing women as a group. The case still stands whether these women 'represent' women or not.

The issues raised in recent feminist discussions of group difference and group representation relate to and extend what has been a long history of debates on democracy, and cannot but concern those who query the inadequacies of what currently passes for political equality. Our societies are not homogeneous: they are structured around systemic inequalities and recurrent exclusions. We exist not just as abstract citizens, but also as members of variously privileged or disadvantaged groups. Political organization based around the dominant cleavages – whether these are by gender or class or ethnicity or religion – is rightly viewed as one possible means of redressing the balance, and my argument in this paper is not against such collective action *per se*. Nor is it an argument against careful consideration of the ways of enhancing group involvement in the process of policy formation and ways of weighting this towards those groups who have been most excluded. And on what seems to me the more straightforward issue of equalizing individuals' access to political elites, I believe the time for reform is long overdue. My reservations refer exclusively to that more ambitious step of institutionalizing group representation, for, in exploring the possible extension of feminist arguments into a case for formal and substantial group representation, I have come to the conclusion that the potential risks outweigh the gains.

Notes

1 Zillah Eisenstein, *The Female Body and the Law* (Berkeley: University of California Press, 1989; Carole Pateman, *The Sexual Contract* (Cambridge: Polity, 1989); Susan Moller Okin *Justice, Gender and the Family* (New York: Basic Books, 1989).

2 Sidney Verba, Norman H. Nie and Jae-on Kim, *Participation and Political Equality* (Cambridge: Cambridge University Press, 1978).

3 For a fuller discussion of the relationship between feminist and democratic theory, see my *Engendering Democracy* (Cambridge: Polity, 1991).

4 See, for example, Irene Diamond and Nancy Hartsock, 'Beyond interests in politics: a comment on Virginia Sapiro's "When are interests interesting?"',

American Political Science Review, 75, 3 (1981); Anna G. Jonasdottir, 'On the concept of interests, women's interests, and the limitations of interest theory', *The Political Interests of Gender*, in ed. K. B. Jones and A. G. Jonasdottir (London: Sage, 1988); Rosemary Pringle and Sophie Watson, ' "Women's interests" and the post-structuralist state', in *Destabilizing Theory: Contemporary Feminist Debates*, ed. Michèle Barrett and Anne Phillips (Cambridge: Polity; Stanford, CT: Stanford University Press, 1992).

5 Benjamin Barber, *Strong Democracy: Participatory Politics for a New Age* (Berkeley: University of California Press, 1984). For an earlier argument that follows similar lines, see Sheldon Wolin, *Politics and Vision* (Boston: Little, Brown, 1960). I discuss the arguments of this 'civic republicanism' more fully in *Engendering Democracy*.

6 Iris Marion Young, 'Polity and group difference: a critique of the ideal of universal citizenship', *Ethics*, 99 (1989), p. 261.

7 Will Kymlicka, *Liberalism, Community and Culture* (Oxford: Clarendon Press, 1989), p. 258.

8 Ibid., p. 50.

9 Ibid., p. 147.

10 Young, 'Polity and group difference', p. 261.

11 Iris Marion Young, 'The ideal of community and the politics of difference', in *Feminism/Postmodernism*, ed. Linda Nicholson (London: Routledge, 1990).

12 Richard A. Joseph, *Democracy and Prebendal Politics in Nigeria* (Cambridge: Cambridge, University Press, 1987).

13 Torild Skard and Elina Haavio-Mannila, 'Mobilization of women at elections', in *Unfinished Democracy: Women in Nordic Politics*, ed. Elina Haavio-Mannila et al. (Oxford: Pergamon Press, 1985).

14 Torild Skard and Elina Haavio-Mannila, 'Women in parliament', in *Unfinished Democracy*.

15 Joni Lovenduski, *Women and European Politics: Contemporary Feminism and Public Policy* (Brighton: Wheatsheaf, 1986), p. 152.

16 At its 1990 conference, for example, the Labour Party finally committed itself to the principle of quotas to achieve at least 40 per cent female representation at all levels within the party, and to the aim of parity between the sexes in the Parliamentary Labour Party over the next ten years or the next three general elections. But there are as yet no agreed mechanisms for achieving the latter – no simple matter within the framework of single member constituencies and local constituency choice.

17 For a critique of the racial dualism of 'black' and 'white', see Tariq Modood, *Not Easy Being British: Colour, Culture and Citizenship* (Stoke on Trent: Trentham Books, 1992).

6

Must Feminists Give up on Liberal Democracy?

Feminism has often found itself at odds with liberal democracy: indeed feminist judgements in this area have usually been harsher than our judgements on liberalism *per se*. Despite many and much rehearsed limitations, liberalism can at least claim credit in the historical development of the feminist tradition, and it enjoys today its double legacy as founding inspiration and favourite target of attack. Liberal *democracy*, by contrast, does not even inspire us. The prolonged exclusion of women from the most basic right to vote turned out to be the merest tip of the iceberg: a discouraging hint at deeper structures that keep women politically unequal. Whatever its claims in other fields of endeavour, liberal democracy has not served women well.[1]

Within this generally damning perspective, there are nonetheless two discernible strands.[2] The first stems from the politics of the contemporary women's movement, which emerged out of a period of widespread dissatisfaction with the banalities of liberal democracy, and shared with virtually all radical groupings of the 1960s and 1970s a vision of a more active, participatory democracy. In the practices of most women's groups, this translated into a distrust of hierarchy and leadership, a concern with sharing expertise and influence and time, and a preference for the direct democracy of the meeting rather than the anonymity of the vote. The relationship between these principles of self-organization and the principles that should govern the polity as a whole were hardly a matter of urgent concern, but, under the broad slogan of 'the personal is political', feminists developed an analysis of power as all-pervasive and democracy as everywhere significant. The women's movement then became associated with the values of local, decentralized democracy, with the idea that democracy matters wherever there are relations of power, and with the importance of organizational forms as prefiguring ultimate goals.

The theorization of feminist perspectives on democracy lagged considerably behind, and as these developed (largely in the course of the 1980s) they moved onto what might seem the more respectable ground of citizenship and political equality.[3] Where the first moment in feminist thinking had coincided with an explosion in participatory democracy, the second occurred at a time of growing disdain for the 'fetish of direct democracy'[4] and resurgent confidence in the procedures of liberal democracy. This confidence has not on the whole been shared by feminists, but the transition from participation towards citizenship nonetheless mirrors the movement in radical thought as a whole. In the first phase, feminists concerned themselves with what we might call the micro-level of democracy inside a movement and democracy in everyday life. In the second phase, we have turned to the macro-level of women's membership in the political community: exploring questions of inclusion and exclusion, and dampening down the universalizing pretensions of modern political thought.[5] The first moment almost sidelined more conventional democratic debates. Perhaps the second will in its turn be sidelined, but, in associating itself with the language of citizenship, it occupies more central ground.

There are reasons behind this shift that are distinctive to feminism, but it also reproduces a division that has characterized all the critical literature on liberal democracy. For many democrats, the decisive weakness of liberal democracy is the way it has restricted the scope and intensity of citizen engagement, retreating so far from classical ideals of democracy as to cast some doubt on the use of the term. The more ambitious practices of active and equal involvement in decision-making have given way to a minimalist or, in Benjamin Barber's term, a 'weak' democracy[6] that offers little more than protection against the excesses of what governments might do. The central principle of contemporary democracy is that governments must subject themselves to periodic recall: there must be enough freedom of association and information to promote the organization of a variety of political parties and there must be regular elections in which all adults are permitted to vote. Those who query the limits of this typically argue for more democracy and democracy in more places. The earlier practices of the women's movement fell broadly within this school.

The second major line of attack focuses on the failure to deliver on the promise of political equality. Liberal democracy tends to regard this as adequately met by the equal rights to vote and to stand for election; and in doing so it abstracts from the social and economic conditions that would make this equality effective. Even setting aside issues of gender and race, our unequal access to economic resources combines with our unequal access to knowledge, information and political skills to render us politically (not just socially) unequal. Robert Dahl clearly acknowledges this in his recent magisterial restatement of his views on democracy, and goes so far as to question whether political equality is compatible with the market economy.[7] But as this very example indicates, the promise of political equality has provoked an extensive literature on the obstacles that might stand in its path; and many defenders of 'actually existing democracy' will admit at least some part of the problem. Certainly, since the post-war development of the welfare state, most of those societies that would appear in the roll-call of liberal democracies have come to address various social or economic rights that may be necessary to make citizenship effectively equal. This poses important questions to the current analyses of women and citizenship. Is the differential political treatment of women and men part of the sorry history of liberal democracies, or built into their very foundations? Does liberal democracy have to turn itself into something *other* – an alternative to liberal democracy – in order to deal with sexual inequality? Or can the inadequacies and inequalities be redressed within some future, but still *liberal* democracy?

I explore here the powerful critiques that feminists have developed under the three broad headings of citizenship, participation and heterogeneity; under each heading, I query whether the arguments add up to a case against liberal democracy. The preoccupation with liberal democracy as a totalizing system we must be either 'for' or 'against' proves relatively unhelpful, for it attributes to liberal democracy a greater theoretical fixity than is confirmed by its subsequent history.[8] The 'democratization' of liberal democracy has already moved it a long way from its founding moments: so far indeed that the neo-liberals and neo-conservatives of the 1970s and 1980s cried out against what they saw as an all-too successful democratic subversion.[9] If the precise character of liberal democracy can be formed and re-formed in a process of political contestation, then feminists may have quite enough on their hands in engendering democracy without also worrying about whether the results are still 'liberal democracy'.

Citizenship

Recent explorations of women and citizenship share considerable common ground with other critiques of liberal democracy, in that they address the substantive conditions that would make political equality more than a nice choice of words. The most obvious point of entry here is the extraordinary under-representation of women in the world's political assemblies. All versions of liberal democracy link the right to vote with the right to stand for election – and few are as cavalier as Joseph Schumpeter, who noted in a brief footnote that we are free to compete for political leadership 'in the same sense in which everyone is free to start another textile mill'.[10] It is, however, in considering the imbalance between the proportion of women in the citizen body and the proportion elected to power that the vacuous nature of this particular right is most starkly revealed.[11] The caring responsibilities that most women carry in relation to the young, the sick and the old – not to mention the able-bodied men – act as a powerful practical barrier to their political involvement, while the cultural constructions of politics as a matter primarily for men work to disadvantage those women who still put themselves forward. The results are entirely predictable: with the important exception of the Nordic countries, the women elected to the world's national assemblies make up between 2 and 12 per cent of the whole.

The solutions to this fall roughly into three categories. Some of the problems relate to the sexual division of labour in production and reproduction, and will only finally be resolved when men and women share equally in the full range of paid and unpaid work. Others are associated with the working conditions of politicians, and require major modification to accommodate people who are active parents as well. Others again relate to the 'boy's club' prejudices of party selectorates or voters, which require affirmative action (such as quotas) to boost the election of women. The importance feminists currently attach to the third reflects our sadly realistic assessment of the time it will take to alter the first two, though this may be a case of dealing with the symptoms rather than tackling the underlying cause. It is worth noting, meanwhile, that the literature on women's (under-) representation rarely addresses it as something intrinsic to the nature of liberal democracy.

The more unique move made by recent theorists is to consider the broader collection of rights and responsibilities that *already* underpin liberal democratic notions of citizenship, and the ways in which these have been gendered. Feminists have drawn attention, for example, to the relationship between citizenship and the defence of one's nation, or between citizenship and the work that one does, noting that in both instances the status of women as citizens appears profoundly ambiguous. In much of the late nineteenth- and early twentieth-century battle for women's suffrage, the fact that women did not fight to defend the realm was regarded as a definitive argument. Carole Pateman has noted that part of the counter-argument for extending the vote to women was that, in their role as mothers and educators, they too were performing a public service: that the women who died in childbirth were sacrificing their lives to the nation just as much as the men who died in battle; that the women who devoted their lives to bearing and rearing children were performing tasks without which no society could survive; that this seemingly private activity was as much a qualification for citizenship as going out to work or defending the nation.[12] The troubling legacy from this, she argues, is that men and women were then incorporated into citizenship in decisively different ways: men primarily as soldiers and workers, women primarily as mothers.

Similar points have been made in relation to the development of the welfare state. In most post-war liberal democracies, the meaning of citizenship was expanded to embrace what are classed as 'social rights', such that a citizen could legitimately expect to be provided with access to education and employment, and, failing that, a living income. Yet the welfare state that supposedly encapsulated this wider citizenship was typically founded around a model of the male as breadwinner responsible for dependent wife and children, and social security provision in Britain, for example, was organized around this conception. Despite subsequent – in my view, largely trivial – changes, the household remains as the unit for calculating social entitlement, and within this household there is a primary/secondary divide. Such practices reflect and help sustain a profoundly gendered division of labour.

The novelty of this argument lies not so much in what is being said about the sexual division of labour, as in the links being forged between the gendered distribution of paid and unpaid labour and the gendered distribution of political status and power. Under the rubric of citizenship, feminists are now exploring issues that used to be dealt with as economic or social policy, and the strategic significance of this is that it lifts the arguments over sexual equality from the private to the public realm. Part of the traditional critique of liberal democracy is that it concedes only the formality of political equality, while ignoring or indeed condoning the social inequalities that are associated with the market economy. The standard riposte is that any of the measures that might be proposed to deal with these 'other' inequalities will come into conflict with liberties that are also part of the democratic tradition: that there is a tension between freedom and equality, and that a balance must be struck between the two.[13] Political equality may not meet all the requirements of an egalitarian society – but then half a cake is always better than none. The more challenging point made in recent feminist explorations is that membership of the political community is itself profoundly gendered. It is not a matter of political equality being *inadequate* – as if this equality has been won, but should now be extended from the political to the social realm – but that our 'political' status as citizens is premised on arrangements of sexual inequality. If men 'earnt' their citizenship as soldiers and workers, while women 'earnt' their citizenship as mothers and educators of their children, then the political settlement has already legitimated the sexual division of labour. The inequalities are intrinsic to the politics, not an extraneous, additional concern.

When equality in the household or at work is conceived as an 'additional' question, then the staunchest supporter of liberal democracy can feel justified in refusing to consider the case. Political equality is one thing; all these other kinds of equality are quite another. No right-thinking democrat would now argue for inequalities in political rights, but democrats can take any position they fancy on what are seen as a range of additional concerns. The demarcation line helps close down discussion of more substantial notions of equality – and, as those following events in East Central Europe have noted, this has particularly disastrous consequences for women. The 1989 revolutions created or restored the rights of citizens to elect their governments; but this has been associated with a reinstatement of women as primarily mothers, with moves to criminalize abortion, shut down child-care facilities, or encourage women out of their full-time jobs.[14] The differential basis on which men and women are incorporated into citizenship is not some historical oddity, but all too alive and well.

These are powerful arguments, but they leave open the question as to how far they challenge the basic principles of liberal democracy. They shift the boundaries between what are public and what are private concerns, and they query the particular point at which this division has been drawn. But while liberal democracies insist on some such boundary (otherwise what does it mean to put 'liberal' in front?), they have proved reasonably flexible in their definitions of where this boundary should lie. Partly under the impact of labour and social democratic parties, liberal democracies have extended the legitimate scope of government interference to include extensive regulation of the workings of the market. And partly under the impact of feminism, they have entered more decisively into the regulation of sexual violence, as in the growing recognition of rape within marriage as a crime. Meanwhile the work of Scandinavian feminists suggests the scope for a new 'social citizenship' that builds care work into the responsibilities of the state.[15] The analysis of unequal citizenship remains as a major and urgent task for anyone concerned with sexual equality. But unless it can be demonstrated that liberal democracy is founded – and not just historically, but in some sense in its very logic – on the differential treatment of women and men, then the work of dealing with this difference may not alter its basic parameters. To argue otherwise would be to establish some central and defining principle that cannot be made compatible with sexual equality. This case is not yet established, and remains an important, but open, question.[16]

Participation

The second major ground for feminist dissatisfaction lies in the critique of liberal democratic minimalism, and the contrast drawn between this and more active participation. Here too there are problems in considering whether the criticisms add up to a case *against* liberal democracy, or more modestly compute as an argument for more democracy within broadly liberal democratic norms. There is an additional difficulty, for women's experience provides evidence on both sides of the argument. While I regard the positive case as stronger, this has to be considered within a balance sheet that moderates the enthusiasm of earlier years.

Let me start with the downside. In a recent overview of feminist writing on citizenship, Kathleen Jones notes that 'feminist ideas about political institutions stress participation almost to the point of obsession':[17] the very phrasing reveals ambivalence towards this kind of obsession. In the course of a powerful argument for a more actively participatory democracy, Iris Marion Young nonetheless warns against the uncritical retention of 'an anarchist, participatory democratic communitarianism to express our vision of the ideal society',[18] and notes the almost overwhelming pressures towards homogeneity that such a politics can bring in its train. As these and other comments indicate, the early practices of direct democracy in the women's movement lent themselves to an overly consensual – indeed illiberal – politics, which made it peculiarly difficult for feminists to agree to disagree. The emphasis on face-to-face meetings encouraged more active and equal participation, but women's groups found it hard to develop the mechanisms for coping with conflict, and particularly in the early years (much less so later on) expected women to discover how fundamentally their interests were shared. The false unities of 'sisterhood' imposed tremendous pressure towards reaching a common consensus, while the almost familial model of political activity exacted 'a toll that is not always consistent with the feminist stress on autonomy and self-development'.[19] Sceptics will recognize this as one of the standard points made in contrasts between liberal and participatory democracy, for liberalism will accept disagreement as inevitable – and certainly not anyone's fault. The more active engagement of participatory democracy often tends towards the opposite, for, instead of taking people and their interests as given, it looks forward to a process of discussion, transformation and change. This is not to say that participatory democracy necessarily anticipates convergence on some 'general will', but in the early years of the contemporary movement such tendencies were undoubtedly strong.

This is one problem feminists have encountered in developing a more active and engaged democracy, serving not so much as a reason for dropping all such ambitions but as a reminder of the problems that direct democracy can bring. The second arises from female rather than feminist experience, and relates to the pressures on women's time. The founding inspiration for all visions of democracy lies back in the fifth century BC, when the citizens of Athens (and other Greek city states) participated in an extraordinarily rich and engaged political life. Citizens did indeed rule, sharing, in however minor a way, in the administrative responsibilities of the city and deciding central matters of legislation and policy in the frequent citizen assemblies. The very intensity of the engagement was, however, at odds with political equality, and the citizen body was severely restricted in size. The most fervent admirer of classical democracy can hardly ignore the premise on which it was founded: the citizens were 'freed' for politics by a vast army of women and foreigners and slaves.

The obvious point made by any contemporary democrat is that citizen assemblies and rotation of duties work only in the context of tiny communities, and do not translate easily to the modern nation state which counts its citizens by the million. In feminist literature, the issue is posed even more starkly, for the very notion of the active citizen presumes someone else is taking care of the children and doing the necessary maintenance of everyday life. In one of the earliest contributions to the now substantial body of feminist political theory, Susan Moller Okin notes that, 'if women were to be politically equal, they, too, would have to spend a considerable amount of time in political meetings and other public activities', which would mean either revising downwards what could be expected of any active citizen, or else substantially socializing the conditions under which child rearing takes place.[20] Current feminist preferences have veered away from purely socialized solutions towards a mixture of increased social provision and equal parenting between women and men. Though this would significantly reduce the burdens on women's time, it is hard to see how anyone would then be 'freed' for citizenship in its grander sense.

Set in this context, the alliance between feminism and participatory democracy looks strained, and, considering the intense pressures on women's time, it is remarkable that feminists have been so wedded to a politics of meetings. We might more readily expect male politicos to warm to a politics of continuous meetings and discussion and debate, all of them held conveniently outside the home and away from the noise of the children. But most women have been so grounded by responsibilities for children and parents and husbands and house that they could well have settled for the less arduous democracy of casting the occasional vote. From Oscar Wilde through to Michael Walzer, people have recurrently worried that activism involves too many meetings: that, whatever the excitements of politics, people also want to 'take long walks, play with their children, paint pictures, make love, and watch television'.[21] Add onto to this rather delightful list the more mundane maintenance that swallows up so much of women's time, and it is astonishing that early feminists sought out the most demanding of democratic forms.

The point can be made more generally to stress the potentially inegalitarian implications of a politics that relies on meetings. Once reformed to include genuinely universal suffrage (and let us not forget how recently this was accomplished), liberal democracy claims to weight all its citizens as equals. In the moment of voting each of us counts only as one. As Philip Green has so acutely observed, this then serves as the definitive answer to any pretensions to greater democracy, for each reference to direct action, to mass protest, to more substantial meeting-based participation exposes itself to the thorny question: who elected *you* to decide?[22] The higher the demands placed on participation, the more inevitable that it will be unevenly spread around; the more active the democratic engagement, the more likely it is to be carried by only a few. The two forms of political participation that are most equally distributed across the populations of contemporary democracies are voting in elections and signing petitions: the two activities, significantly, that demand the least of our time. All other moments of democratic engagement involve groups that are largely self-selecting and were not authorized to speak for the rest. In considering what counts as fair and equal representation, the very weakness of liberal democracy then turns into its strength. Precisely because it sets its demands so low, asking only that we turn up at the polling booth to register an occasional vote, it can anticipate majority involvement. 'In this way the liberal pluralist tradition tends to make elections into virtually absolute trumps: the only legitimate method of ascertaining the will of the only definable cast of characters known as "the People".'[23] All further extensions of democracy can be criticized as unrepresentative.

This is where we must turn to the counter-arguments that press feminism to a more participatory engagement. Liberal democracy takes the high ground of requiring the sanction of the popular vote, but in doing so it fails to engage with the inadequacies of voting as an expression of our interests or needs. Through centuries of contestation, democrats have pointed out that voting once every five years hardly counts as a substantial expression of popular control, that choosing between alternatives that may vary only in detail does not give citizens much of a choice, that choosing between vaguely expressed and all too frequently abandoned programmes leaves the decisions to the political elites. The further problem relates to the vote as an expression of interests. In the analysis of female identity and interests, feminism adds considerable weight to those who have queried this connection.

One of the defining characteristics of women's movement politics was the importance attached to 'consciousness-raising', and the widely shared sense that women were grappling with a contradictory identity they had in some sense been forced to assume. In Simone de Beauvoir's classic statement, 'one is not born a woman, one becomes one', and part of this social construction is precisely a culture of passivity and self-denial.

Women have felt the need to 'unlearn' the lessons of their past: hence the otherwise odd experience of having to 'discover' that women were oppressed. What made this possible was of course the contradictory nature of women's experiences and consciousness, the feeling that things did not fit. But the political problem that flows from this is not so much that women know what they want and have been unable to make themselves heard; even more pervasive and damaging are the difficulties in articulating one's needs. A key implication in terms of democracy is the transformative significance of meetings, discussion, talk. Interests are not already 'there', pre-given or fixed. Democracy is not just about registering (however occasionally) one's existing preferences and views. For women in particular, there is a prior and continuing process of creating one's identity, constructing one's interests and forming one's political views.

Feminists have built on such arguments to query the very notion of a 'women's interest' that can be simply mobilized and expressed;[24] and, if in the earlier years there was a common perception of stripping away the accretions of centuries to find the 'real' person beneath, contemporary theory speaks almost with one voice in regarding female identity as multiple, unstable, something to be created and re-created, rather than simply uncovered. The further one goes in this direction, the more crucial is that vision of wider participation that informs critics of liberal democracy. The inadequacy of the vote is not just that it occurs so infrequently and provides no substantial popular control. As important is its presumption that interests are pre-given, and the way this works to sustain the status quo.[25] The social construction of femininity (by implication, masculinity as well) is such that we cannot simply accept initial positions as expressions of people's interests and needs. The opinions that are registered through elections, referendums or the seemingly endless plethora of opinion polls and attitude surveys are not to be taken as the first and last word, for, when gender so profoundly structures our sense of our selves and our interests, these original positions are ambiguous and suspect.

This first part of the argument for a more active democracy combines with the second point: that feminist analysis of oppression goes beyond material inequalities of income or occupation to focus on women's marginality and lack of power. If sexual inequality reduced itself to the distribution of income and work (too little of the first and far too much of the second) it would in principle lay itself open to remedies from above. Armed with the crucial democratic weapon of the vote, women could work to elect a government more responsive to women's poverty, one committed to a fuller programme of equal pay for equal work, combined with a set of welfare policies that would cater for women's needs. But the problems of oppression are not resolved through redistribution alone, for they involve not merely an unequal end-state in the distribution of goodies, but an institutional context that limits our ability to participate and the development of our own capacities.[26] The kind of autonomy and self-respect that feminism seeks to develop can be arrived at only when women shake off their status as dependants, and this in turn happens only through the activity of women themselves.

For both these reasons, feminism remains committed to a politics of participation, to women's more active involvement in making decisions for themselves. But, once again, the question arises: is this an argument against the principles of liberal democracy, or for further democratization within the framework of liberal democracy? Women's acute sensitivity to the pressures of time joins with feminist experience of pitfalls of direct democracy to block too polarized an alternative between more meetings and just going out to vote, encouraging us to combine the strengths of both traditions rather than setting up one as superior to the other. The problem with liberal democracy may then lie not so much in its being intrinsically incapable of extending forms of citizen participation, as in the complacency with which it claims to have met all legitimate democratic aspirations. Not that this makes it so much easier to deal with. The closure may be historically contingent rather than logically determined, but at a period in history when liberal democrats feel they have won all the political battles, this complacency is a powerful obstacle to further democratization.

Heterogeneity and group difference

The final area of contention may prove the most difficult for liberal democracy to swallow, for it takes issue with the individual as the basic unit in democratic life. If we consider liberal democracy as an amalgam of certain key principles from the liberal and democratic traditions, what it takes from liberalism is an abstract individualism which may note the differences between us, but says these differences should not count. At its best, this is a statement of profound egalitarianism that offers all citizens the same legal and political rights, regardless of their wealth, status, race or sex. At its worst, it refuses the pertinence of continuing difference and inequality, pretending for the purposes of argument that we are all of us basically the same. Feminists working on issues of legal or economic equality have noted how difficult this can make it for women to press for any differential treatment that may be necessary for significant equality. Feminists working on issues of democratic representation have come up against the same kind of problems, most notably in arguing that the sex of our representatives matters.

As recent experience in the Nordic countries has shown, the under-representation of women is entirely open to remedy – and even without that much needed upheaval that would redistribute work more equally between women and men. With sufficient political will, aided by formal party quotas to ensure a 40 per cent minimum for either sex, the numbers of women elected as political representatives can be dramatically raised. That political will materializes, however, only when gender is acknowledged as a salient political factor. The abstract individualism of liberal democracy is a powerful impediment to this, for it encourages a notion of the 'individual' and 'citizen' as a character of indifferent sex. In societies that are thoroughly saturated by gender, such indifference to sex can only reinforce the position of men.

Recent feminist work has pushed this insight further, building on the analysis of sexual difference to develop far-reaching arguments that deal with the multiple group differences of heterogeneous societies, and the ways these can be represented and expressed. The starting point, for example, of Iris Young's critique of existing democracy is that it fails to admit the pertinence of group differentiation.[27] Liberal democracy presumes a continuing plurality of opinions and beliefs (as its insistence on multi-party competition confirms), but, with the exception of what have come to be known as consociational democracies, it does not see this plurality as relating to different, and unequal, social groups. Political parties address us as people with varying opinions on the major national issues of the day, and, though these parties will frequently draw their support from distinct class groupings, the aggregate has to be broad enough (and vague enough) to contest a national election. Pressure groups can of course mobilize on a more particular social basis (black parents for better schools, students for higher grants, farmers for larger subsidies) but then the very particularity works against them, for they are only one among many competing interests. The question raised in Iris Young's work is whether political equality can be meaningful without formal mechanisms for representing group difference.

The vitality of democracy, she argues, cannot wait on us to settle whether such group differentiation is desirable or inevitable (though she herself believes it is both of these things). 'Our political problem is that some of our groups are privileged and others are oppressed.'[28] Existing mechanisms deliver effective power to the dominant groups, and, while their dominance may be dressed up in the trappings of an impartial general perspective or presented as just the majority decision mobilized through a national vote, the consequence is the continued suppression of any marginalized, disadvantaged voice. Democracy cannot continue to proceed on the assumption of an undifferentiated humanity, or the complacent assertion that voices are equally weighted by their equal right to participate in the vote.

The alternative agenda Young proposes would provide for public funding to promote the self-organization of oppressed groups; establish a requirement on policy-makers that they take into consideration the policy proposals that then emanate from such groups; and, most controversial of all, supply a veto power over specific policies that most directly affect any of these groups. I do not present this as a blueprint for the future – the debate on it has barely commenced – and indeed have several reservations on the notion of group representation. These include the difficult problems of group closure (people coming to define themselves politically through what is only one frozen single aspect of their lives); the question of who is to legislate on which groups qualify for additional group representation; and the almost insuperable obstacles to establishing what any group wants. I have dealt with these at greater length elsewhere;[29] the most pertinent in this context is how to develop acceptably democratic procedures for mobilizing any group voice. After centuries of experimentation, we have only two tried and tested procedures. People can cast their votes in some anonymous ballot, or can turn up at meetings in order to express their views. The first seems particularly inappropriate to the development of a hitherto marginalized perspective, for how are we to identify all the relevant constituents, and how make sure they are voting with that particular part of their identity in mind? (One could feasibly organize all women onto a women's register, but could not expect them all to be voting *as women*, rather than as Catholics or as socialists or as people with some other axe to grind. With smaller, and less visible, sub-groupings, it is hard even to know who makes up the group.) The alternative is to rely on the meeting, which has the double advantage of leaving it to the group members to identify themselves, and enabling them to develop a group perspective. But the slightest acquaintance with studies of political participation confirms what most of us know already from personal experience of meetings: that those who go to meetings are a tiny proportion of the potential group.

The issue of group inequality is far too serious to be brushed aside by any such reservations as these. The questions of democracy and difference are ones that lie at the heart of contemporary dilemmas in democracy – and, on an international scale, have their counterpart in the fragmentation of older empires into smaller nationalities and the rising threat to national minorities. People do not define themselves just as citizens of a nation but, either through choice or necessity, often identify with some smaller sub-group. Where this reflects a history of systematic ill-treatment for particular minorities, it cannot be summarily dismissed as an irrelevant basis for democratic organization. But the mechanisms we are offered to deal with systemic group difference and inequality often look like the old interest-group politics dressed up in more radical guise. Iris Young's vision of an active and grass-roots representation for oppressed groups looks a good deal more promising than the elitist practices of consociational democracies – but still does not resolve all problems. As those who speak in the older language of civic republicanism rightly remind us, democracy also includes a vision of people coming to perceive the limits of their own specific interests and concerns, learning to recognize the potential conflicts between their own position and that adopted by others, and acknowledging the wider community to which we all ultimately belong. This vision has usually failed – it has never proved comprehensive enough to embrace all specific group interests or articulate all grassroots concerns – but this is not enough to dislodge it from its place in the democratic tradition. Perhaps the worst legacy of the Thatcherite years in Britain has been the way they legitimated a politics of individual and narrow group interest, scorning the idealism of all those who contributed to the more generous visions of the modern welfare state. And while this lays itself open to a powerful critique in terms of the *other* interests that have been discarded or denied – primarily those in the lowest income brackets in society – it is even more fundamentally at odds with any notion that there might be common concerns.

Feminists have their own experience of this, which surfaces in exasperation that we must continue to articulate 'the women's point of view' when this is only one of many burning concerns. What inspires this is not just a fear of being kept on the sidelines (the fear expressed by many women politicians throughout this century who have resisted association with 'women's issues' as something that would keep them from the centres of power) but a more profound sense that politics is about a whole range of issues and visions which do not reduce to group interest or need. In this sense, one of the major problems in developing a feminist vision of democracy is how to resist the pressures towards subsuming women under the supposedly gender-neutral 'man' without thereby capitulating to the narrowness of merely group interest or need. Or, to put it the other way round, how to retain a vision of human beings working democratically together in pursuit of their shared concerns, without falling into the complacency that dismisses the systematic inequalities between groups?

What is important here is that liberal democracy as currently practised makes it hard even to address this dilemma, for it recurrently returns us to the individual as the basic unit in political life, blocking serious consideration of the empowerment of disadvantaged *groups*. This is perhaps the point of most marked divergence between feminist and liberal democratic perspectives, and, as feminist theorists pursue the complex and difficult implications of a 'politics of difference', we can anticipate considerable resistance from those who see democracy in relentlessly individual terms. The question then is whether these hardy individualists exhaust the possibilities of liberal democracy, whether such individualism is intrinsic to its nature? It is hard to give a definitive 'yes'. Michael Walzer has recently reformulated the communitarian critiques of liberalism as a debate *within* liberalism;[30] Will Kymlicka has set out an impeccably liberal case for recognizing group rights;[31] while the current practices of consociational democracies already provide institutionalized representation for communities as well as individuals. Unless we define these theoretical and political initiatives as outside the scope of liberal democracy, then liberal democracy has already made gestures towards recognizing the pertinence of the group.

Feminism and liberal democracy

These three areas indicate both the extent of feminist dissatisfaction with existing liberal democracy and the problems in resolving whether this adds up to an alternative view. Feminist explorations of citizenship raise major questions about the basis on which women have been included in the political community, and consider the substantive conditions that have to be met in order to qualify for political equality. The weight feminism attaches to women being able to transform their identity and sense of themselves highlights the continuing importance of active involvement in collective discussion and action. The critique of dependency as a crucial part of sexual inequality puts feminism firmly in the camp of a strong democracy, where what matters is empowerment as well as the ultimate policy results. The analysis of systemic inequalities – not only between women and men, but more generally between oppressed and dominant social groups – raises important questions about empowering people not only as individuals but also as members of specific groups.

Each of these pinpoints what has been a recurrent feature of liberal democracy, and the arguments combine in an enduring and radical critique of the limits of existing democracy. Yet none of them can be presented as a decisive alternative to liberal democracy, partly because of the difficulties in disentangling what are historical origins from what is defining essence. Origins do not shape all subsequent developments, and establishing either the historical – or, as feminists are well able to do, the contemporary – associations between liberal democracy and sexual inequality does not prove a necessary or intrinsic connection. A richer and more equal democracy may still be possible within the broad framework liberal democracy implies.

When the world is littered with the skeletons of 'alternatives' to liberal democracy, it is particularly difficult to present one's critique as leading to a qualitatively different political form. Thus feminists may – I believe should – associate themselves with the impetus towards a more active and engaged democracy; but we cannot afford to present this as an alternative to holding elections. Feminists have always challenged – and will continue to challenge – the way that particular divisions between the public and private secure the exclusion and oppression of women; but few would want to build on this to argue for dissolving all such distinctions. Feminists are rightly extending the analysis of sexual difference into a wider consideration of the systematic differences between unequal social groups; but the requirements of democratic accountability combine with the reservations over 'merely' group interest and need to set some cautionary limits to this.

Caution is of course the watchword of the moment, and the more likely danger for the immediate future lies less in the risk of non-democratic alternatives to liberal democracy than in the complacency of those who feel they have reclaimed the political agenda. In both its theory and its practice, liberal democracy has largely failed to engage with sexual equality, and it would be a sorry outcome for democracy in general if the extraordinary political events of the 1980s and 1990s ushered in a period of unquestioning celebration of the limited democracy we currently enjoy. It is indeed against this background that I worry about the shift in emphasis from participation towards citizenship. However shaky the democracy of the meeting, however exposed to the taunt that too few people will go, the more active and engaged democracy that was practised in the early years of the women's movement cannot be dislodged from feminist notions of a better and fuller democracy. The trump card of elections, of guaranteeing the numerical equality that gives each individual an equal weight, has to be seen in this context. It serves as a crucial reminder of the founding and abiding principle of democracy – that in democracy we are meant to be equals – and introduces a necessary caution into all our discussions about developing and deepening democracy. But premised as it still is on a notion that interests or preferences are unproblematic, and working as it always does to discourage more radical innovation, it cannot be taken as the simple last word. It does not help to discuss these issues in terms of an 'alternative' to liberal democracy, but, for all the reasons outlined above, feminism will continue to inspire a more substantial democracy than that which is currently on offer.

Notes

1 Among the critical literature, see Carole Pateman, 'Feminism and democracy' (1983), repr. in Pateman, *The Disorder of Women* (Cambridge: Polity, 1990); Sheila Rowbotham, 'Feminism and democracy', in *New Forms of Democracy*, ed. D. Held and C. Pollitt (Milton Keynes: Open University Press: London: Sage, 1986); Anne Phillips, *Engendering Democracy* (Cambridge: Polity, 1991).
2 I restrict myself here to feminist engagement with liberal democracy over the twenty-five years since the contemporary women's movement was born. Other stories can be told of earlier feminist engagements.
3 For an overview of more recent literature, see Kathleen B. Jones, 'Citizenship in a woman-friendly polity', *Signs*, 15, 4 (1990).
4 Norberto Bobbio, *Which Socialism?* (Cambridge: Polity, 1986), p. 78.
5 For feminist critiques of universalizing theory, see Carole Pateman, *The Sexual Contract* (Cambridge: Polity, 1988); essays in Linda Nicholson (ed.), *Feminism/Postmodernism* (London Routledge, 1990); and ch. 3.

6   Benjamin Barber, *Strong Democracy: Participatory Politics for a New Age* (Berkeley: University of California Press, 1984).

7   'If democracy is to exist and citizens are to be political equals, then will democracy not require something other than a market-oriented, private enterprise economy, or at the very least a pretty drastic modification of it?' Robert Dahl, *Democracy and its Critics* (New Haven, CT: Yale University Press, 1989), p. 326.

8   I am indebted to David Beetham for the remarks that finally liberated me from this preoccupation.

9   This is argued in Ernesto Laclau and Chantal Mouffe, *Hegemony and Socialist Strategy* (London: Verso, 1985), ch. 4.

10 Joseph A. Schumpeter, *Capitalism, Socialism and Democracy* (London: Allen & Unwin, 1954), p. 272n.

11 For a recent overview of conditions throughout the world, see Vicky Randall, *Women and Politics* (2nd edn, London: Macmillan, 1987). For a fuller discussion of the issues of representation, see Phillips, *Engendering Democracy*, ch. 3.

12 Carole Pateman, talk on work in progress, Gender Group, London School of Economics, 26 April 1991. See also her 'Equality, difference, subordination: the politics of motherhood and women's citizenship', in *Beyond Equality and Difference*, ed. G. Bock and S. James (London: Routledge, 1992).

13 Steven Lukes has argued persuasively that this formulation is inadequate: that the trade-offs are not between equality on the one hand and liberty on the other, but between different combinations or interpetations of both. See 'Equality and liberty: must they conflict?', in *Political Theory Today*, ed. David Held (Cambridge: Polity, 1991).

14 See, for example, Barbara Einhorn, 'Where have all the women gone? Women and the women's movement in East Central Europe', *Feminist Review*, 39 (1991).

15 See Birte Siim, 'Towards a feminist rethinking of the welfare state', in *The Political Interests of Gender*, in ed. K. B. Jones and A. G. Jonasdottir (London: Sage, 1988).

16 This parallels that other major question that must be put to liberal democracy: what is the relationship between democracy and the market? Is the market historically contingent or a condition without which liberal democracy cannot possibly thrive? See Christopher Pierson, 'Democracy, markets and capital: are there necessary economic limits to democracy?', *Political Studies*, 40 (1992).

17 Jones, 'Citizenship in a woman-friendly polity', p. 788.

18 Iris Marion Young, 'The ideal of community and the politics of difference', in *Feminism/Postmodernism*, ed. Linda Nicolson (London: Routledge, 1990), p. 301.

19 Jones, 'Citizenship in a woman-friendly polity', p. 808.

20 Susan Moller Okin, *Women in Western Political Thought* (London: Virago, 1980), p. 278.

21 Michael Walzer, 'A day in the life of a socialist citizen', in *Obligations: Essays on Disobedience, War and Citizenship* (Cambridge, MA: Harvard University Press, 1970), p. 234.

22 Philip Green, 'A review essay of Robert A. Dahl *Democracy and Its Critics*', *Social Theory and Practice*, 16, 2 (1990).

23 Ibid., p. 238.

24 See Rosemary Pringle and Sophie Watson, ' "Women's interests" and the post-structuralist state', in *Destabilizing Theory: Contemporary Feminist Debates*, ed. Michèle Barrett and Anne Phillips (Cambridge: Polity, 1992).

25 There is a parallel here with the arguments developed in Benjamin Barber's *Strong Democracy*, which similarly emphasizes the transformative significance of active participation through meetings. Note, however, that aspects of his argument have been roundly criticized from a feminist perspective by Iris Young in her essay on 'Polity and group difference'.

26 Iris Marion Young, *Justice and the Politics of Difference* (Princeton, NJ: Princeton University Press, 1990).

27 Young, *Justice and the Politics of Difference*; see also 'Polity and group difference: a critique of the ideal of universal citizenship', *Ethics*, 99 (1989).

28 Young, 'Polity and group difference', p. 261.

29 Chapter 5.

30 Michael Walzer, 'The communitarian critique of liberalism', *Political Theory*, 18, 1 (1990).

31 Will Kymlicka, *Liberalism, Community and Culture* (Oxford: Clarendon Press, 1989).

7

The Promise of Democracy

In suggesting that democracy holds out a promise – and by implication that it has so far failed to deliver – I am already going against a strain of tough-minded realism that has worked hard through much of this century to free us from utopian dreams. Twentieth-century discussion of democracy has tended to dampen down the talk of promise. We might think here of Max Weber – the 'liberal in despair'[1] who anticipated the increasing power of both private and public bureaucracies, and who came to view democracy as essentially a means of selecting competent leaders – or Robert Michels – the democratic socialist who came to believe that all organizations would fall under the iron law of oligarchy.[2] But these were worriers, people who came reluctantly to their pessimistic conclusions. More straightforwardly, we might think of someone like Joseph Schumpeter, whose brief chapters on democracy in his 1942 *Capitalism, Socialism and Democracy* set out what was to become a dominant theme in later discussions.[3]

Schumpeter identified what he saw as a classical notion of democracy which promised what could not be delivered, and warned us off this misleading ideal. The key illusion for Schumpeter was the belief in a 'common good' or a 'general will', which would emerge when the people were gathered together to make their political decisions. He regarded this as nonsense – for a variety of reasons, including irreconcilable value differences, human irrationality in matters of politics (he thought – and perhaps with some justification – that we all had a reduced sense of reality and responsibility when it came to political decisions), and what he saw as the immense scope for manipulation of human interests and desires.

Subsequent theorists have echoed or embroidered this general theme of promises that cannot be met. Giovanni Sartori, for example (scourge of the democratic left for thirty-odd years), complains that the ideals of democracy have remained very much what they were in the fourth century BC, when the citizens of Athens were still able to meet together in a single assembly and directly govern themselves, and when there was no real sense in which some people were being represented by others.[4] Despite all the subsequent changes in the organization of social life, the principal values of democracy have persisted in this ancient mould, and still address a direct democracy. Thus, as he puts it, 'the astounding fact ... that we have created a representative democracy – performing a near miracle that Rousseau still declared impossible – without value-support.'[5] It is time, Sartori suggests, for a quick fix in value-management; time to bring our ideals more in line with reality.

These arguments are not without substance. The early democracy of the Greek city states was premised on geographically limited and socially homogeneous communities, in which it was just about feasible to talk of all citizens participating directly in the management of their affairs, and just about coherent to expect these citizens to reach a political consensus. But as the geographical boundaries of the political community shifted from the city state to the nation state – and now indeed towards cross-national communities such as Europe – then any dreams of the citizenry as actively combining together in the administration of their society began to seem thoroughly naive. More poignantly still, as we have broken the exclusivity of the citizens, as we have insisted on extending the rights of participation to the unpropertied, to women, to those who were once slaves, we have not only enlarged, but also complicated, the citizen body – we have made it far more heterogeneous.

To this extent, at least, the realists have a point. It would seem that it is no longer possible to deliver on two of the founding promises of democracy: neither active citizen participation in the making of the laws, nor dedication to any unifying common purpose. Democracy as we now know it emerged through a dual shift – from direct to representative democracy, and from a politics of the common good to a politics of individual protection. 'The gradual shift', as Michael Sandel describes it, 'from the public philosophy of common purposes to one of fair procedures, from a politics of good to a politics of rights, from the national republic to the procedural republic'.[6] Democracy has become less a matter of active citizenship and more a matter of fair-dos. Expectations have been reduced, earlier promises have been cancelled. It seems anachronistic to ask for anything more.

I have argued elsewhere[7] that the vision of a more active and sub-stantial democracy cannot be dislodged from feminist ideals, and that the crucial inadequacies of the vote as an expression of interests require us to continue our exploration of ways of enhancing participation and discussion. But let me sidestep for the moment this terrain on which the realists do battle with those they regard as utopians, and focus on one major qualification which undercuts the prevailing image of democracy as a historic retreat. The first promises of direct participation in the promotion of a common good may indeed have been whittled away, but they have been supplanted by a far more youthful promise of demo-cratic equality. Though equality is sometimes taken almost as a syn-onym for democracy today, it played a very subordinate role in the classical ideals. The Greek city states in the fifth or fourth century BC may have insisted on equality between citizens, but they had no qualms about excluding women and slaves, and even when it came to free-born men they operated pretty tight controls. The Athenian assembly, for example, decided to exclude any man who could not demonstrate Athenian descent on both his father's and mother's side; and Pericles, who was responsible for proposing this restriction, later had to plead for a waiver for his own illegitimate sons, whose mother came from Asia Minor. (He wouldn't, of course, have bothered if his fully qualified, legitimate sons hadn't died of plague.)[8]

The ancient Greeks did not see democracy as promising a more gen-eral human equality, and it is interesting, in this context, that it was the *anti*-democratic Plato who queried the exclusion of women from politics, and considered them as legitimate candidates for his elite of Guardians. The relationship between democracy and equality took a long time to develop, and was still not particularly intimate in the second great moment of democratic transformation which began in seventeenth-century Europe. At that point in time, men of property began to chal-lenge the authoritarian powers of their rulers, refused any longer to consider such powers as ordained by God or tradition, and started to explore the alternative notion that government must be based on consent. The early images of the free-born consenting citizen were pretty limited in their reference and scope – they certainly did not mean anything like the equal right of all adults to vote – but, fortunately for all of us, ideas have a logic of their own. As this particular idea gathered pace through eighteenth-century declarations of the Rights of Man, through the turbulent days of the French Revolution, and on into the nineteenth- and twentieth-century battles over the suffrage, democracy came to imply a far more generous citizen equality. The notion of democratic consent was painfully but successively detached from its origins in either property or masculinity.[9] The rights of man inspired the rights of woman; and the arguments over suffrage were pushed to their limits, till neither class nor gender nor race could be admitted as grounds for denying people their equal right to vote.

It is salutary to remember how recent this admission was. It was not until 1971, for example, that Switzerland finally admitted women's equal right to vote – and I can still recall, as a politics undergraduate, being encouraged to discuss the thorny question of whether it would be such a good idea for Switzerland to give women the vote, when all the evidence suggested they would then vote in more conservative governments.[10] In the United States of America, it was not until the civil rights campaigns of the 1950s and 1960s that black people were able to register their right to vote on the same basis as white people. Meanwhile, in the 1980s and 1990s, commentators on the political situation in South Africa still discuss developments in terms of 'one man, one vote'.

As a serious political initiative, the promise of democratic equality has only just made the agenda, and in this sense is very unlike the other promises associated with democracy. The predominant theme of twentieth-century discussions has been that we must come to terms with reality, that we must abandon the anachronisms of the classical ideals, recognize the limits of democracy, cut our values to the sorry shape of the world. But as far as equality is concerned, we have only just begun to explore the democratic promise.

Democracy in the 1980s and 1990s

Now it might seem that this is a particularly propitious time for such further exploration, for this is meant to be the great moment of democratic revival, when democracy has returned to the centre of the political stage. 1989 is commonly regarded as a watershed year: the year when one-party rule crumbled throughout East-Central Europe, when, in one country after another, people mobilized to dismiss the ruling communists from their monopoly of power and to replace them through competitive elections; also, of course, the year when the Chinese Communist Party had to resort to brutal suppression of popular demonstration in order to retain its control (and it is hard to believe that that's the last we'll hear of Chinese democracy). Meanwhile, in Latin America, the 1980s witnessed one military regime after another handing over power to an elected government; in sub-Saharan Africa, the same years brought a crisis in legitimacy – if not yet in power – for the post-colonial one-party states; in South Africa, there is what must now be an unstoppable impetus towards the democracy of one-person, one-vote.

I could pile on the rhetoric, but there is always something a bit suspect in the grand patterns we impose on history. Francis Fukuyama's *The End of History and the Last Man* is a particularly noteworthy reminder here: a book which proclaims, more recklessly than most, the world historic defeat of any alternatives to liberal democracy. In a recent review of this work, Alan Ryan notes wryly that nine years previously there was a very different book published, to equally widespread acclaim, entitled *How Democracies Perish*. 'At that time, many people pointed out that they weren't perishing in any great number, but M. Revel was not much deterred . . . Now we have Mr. Fukuyama telling us that democracies not only do not perish, but are inscribed in History.'[11] If you want to write a best seller, you would be well advised to claim either that democracies are perishing, or that they are taking over the world; outside of publishers' blurbs, history tends to be a bit more messy.

We should not then get carried away by the notion that this is an extraordinary moment in the history of democracy. But even if we turn more modestly and more locally to Britain, there does seem to be something in the image of the 1980s as a period of revival for democratic ideas and campaigns. Growing disquiet over the arrogance of government and infringements of individual liberties has combined with the increasingly marked anomalies of the British electoral system to renew debate on the inadequacies of British democracy. There is now a significantly higher level of popular concern and popular legitimacy for reforms of the electoral system, for abolition of a hereditary House of Lords, for the introduction of a Bill of Rights, perhaps even for the disestablishment of the monarchy. Issues of democracy are entering more fully into mainstream political debate in Britain – and this is quite a novel phenomenon.

Yet on both the global *and* the local level, the debates over democracy range far less widely than they did in the past. These are indeed rather odd times for democracy: for just as democracy becomes a more central and widespread preoccupation, so we have retreated from much of democracy's grander 'promise'. The debate in 1980s and 1990s Britain, for example, has been very much driven by constitutional argument: the powers of government to be reined in by a fairer electoral system; the fragility of individual freedoms to be shored up by a Bill of Rights interpreted by a wise judiciary; the absurdities of the House of Lords to be replaced by an elected second chamber – each proposal, significantly, is based on existing practice in some part of the existing liberal democratic world. We are no longer addressing what might be more fundamental contradictions, inequities, or just plain failures of imagination; we are no longer exploring the gap between the promises and the realities of democracy; we seem to be talking about how to spread the best of current practices more widely around. So for the new states of East-Central Europe to become more like the democracies of West Europe; for Britain to approximate more closely the democracy of the United States: compared to the 'promises' implicit in democracy, these are oddly limited ambitions.

What of those other questions that continued to bother democrats throughout this century – and in particular, that mountain of evidence and discussion which has dealt with the relationship between economic and political equality? The pressures from the realists may have dampened down expectations of direct democracy, but they did little to discourage anxiety over the tensions between class and citizenship, and did not erase troubled explorations of the way that economic inequality is reproduced and reinforced in levels of political participation and influence. I am thinking here not only of socialist arguments on the incompatibility between the market and democracy,[12] but also of the more sober and respectable discussions in post-war Britain that conceived of citizenship as a combination of civil, political and *social* rights;[13] and indeed the material from the heartland of American political science that has shown how those with more economic and educational resources also turn about to be those with greater access to the political arena.[14] What has happened to these wider issues of political equality?

The question is rhetorical, for of course we know what has happened to these. The decade that put democracy more firmly on the political map was simultaneously the decade that shattered so much of the basis for socialist – even to some extent social-democratic – critiques. The combined crises of welfarism and communism have taken their toll, and in some senses rightly so. In particular, the arguments between socialists and liberals too often took shape not so much in different readings of the democratic promise, as in what came rather close to an opposition between equality and democracy. Socialists focused on the substantive inequalities in the social and economic order, and seemed willing to risk the political authoritarianism that might be involved in measures to eradicate them; while liberals focused on democracy and freedoms and rights, and would not tolerate further growth in public power. Those who took the socialist side in this debate would almost certainly query the assumption that greater economic equality brings with it lesser individual freedom and a more powerful state; those who took the liberal side would accuse the critics of wishful thinking.

This particular argument has reached a (temporary?) cul-de-sac, not, I believe, because the market has proved itself the great guarantor of democratic freedoms and equalities, but because people have lost confidence in arguments that rely on some grand historical version of 'everything turning out all right on the night'. Wishful thinking has little to recommend it in a world that has witnessed the collapse of so many self-proclaimed 'alternatives', and people are rightly distrustful of arguments that refuse to engage with potential conflicts between equality and democracy. There is a much more cautious mood in the air. The notion that we can have all the things we might desire of a better society – and have them all together – smacks too much of utopianism: the dominant trend is towards recognizing difficult choices between what may be equally desirable but perhaps incompatible ends.

New issues of democracy

Against this more sombre background, the troubled relationship between class and citizenship has slipped off the democratic agenda. I do not myself anticipate these questions disappearing for ever (and am heartened in this respect to note that Robert Dahl expects the relationship between economic and political equality to be at the centre of the next democratic transformation).[15] These issues are too much part of the democratic promise to go away for ever, but I shall leave them where they are for the present. What I want to do for the rest of my discussion is to turn to the newer issues of democratic equality that arise in the context of a plural society.

What I have in mind here are the fledgling initiatives towards recognizing the dominance of particular social groups and perspectives within what are plural and heterogeneous societies, and the attempts to counter this dominance by increasing the representation of groups that were previously excluded. There is a growing debate around what is called the politics of difference, or the politics of diversity, where people are challenging what they have come to see as the phony generalities that shelter far more particular concerns. Feminists have been going on for a long time about the masculine bias in our supposedly gender-neutral notions of humanity; black groups have taken issue with the assimilationism that tries to mould all communities in the image of the white majority; at a more specific level, many have queried the Eurocentric bias that influences the curriculum in higher education, and the way that the new national curriculum being developed for British schools reasserts a very British – not to say English – version of 'our' common history. All these initiatives signal a different set of problems in the practices of contemporary democracy, suggesting that the political agenda is too much weighted to the concerns of dominant – and not even majority – groups.

The appalling under-representation of women and members of ethnic minority communities in our political assemblies is only the tip of this iceberg. The issues then spread out more widely to touch on profoundly uncomfortable questions such as the rights of different religious communities to order their children's education as they see fit, or the need to adapt our understanding of legal equality so that it no longer means everyone being treated exactly the same, or the desirability of additional group representation for those whose interests have been marginal to the political agenda.

It is not, I believe, too much of an exaggeration to say that disagreements over what constitutes equal citizenship in a plural and divided society are now central to political debates in the United States: they were certainly central to the basis on which Pat Buchanan challenged George Bush for the 1992 Republican nomination; it has been plausibly argued that they were central to the political crisis in the 1980s in support for the Democratic Party.[16] And though these arguments have usually focused on the role of affirmative action programmes in education and employment, they are ultimately about what kind of democracy is appropriate and possible in a country where the lines of inequality coincide far too closely with ethnic and linguistic division. In British politics, related questions have surfaced most directly in the numerous local government initiatives of the 1980s which sought to establish some mechanism of representation for groups whose specific needs had been inadequately addressed. Thus the decision by many local authorities to establish women's committees or women's units, anti-racist committees or ethnic minorities units, or to appoint officers with special responsibility for disadvantaged groups. Much of this work was focused on employment practices within the various councils – and to that extent also comes more under the rubric of equal opportunities in employment than the representation of otherwise marginalized prespectives – but most of it also implies a critique of our over-generalized, emptily-abstract citizenship.

Such initiatives assume, for example, that the mechanisms of party competition are too crude to ensure adequate representation for all legitimate group interests, that too many groups slip through this particular democratic net. None of the political parties (at either national or local level) can be relied upon to speak forcefully or consistently on a range of so-called women's issues, or to articulate the needs and concerns of communities that are in an ethnic or religious minority. At its simplest, this is because too few politicians come from these 'minorities' – minorities, of course, that add up to a clear majority of the citizen body. More elusively, it is because the dominant political culture still operates within an essentially unitary paradigm, a framework that tends to silence – or disparage – the voices of those who are different.

I will not address here the question of whether these inequalities are more or less important than class inequalities, nor say anything in particular about the relationship between the two kinds of concerns (except just to note in passing that there *is* a relationship – as measured in the crudest of indicators, such as the high levels of unemployment among Afro-Caribbean men in Britain and African-American men in the United States, or the preponderance of women among low paid workers). The point I would stress is that *these* questions of political equality add a new dimension to the older anxieties about structural social inequality, for they deal with groups from which you cannot or do not want to escape. Women neither can nor want to change their sex, nor black people the colour of their skin, in order to win equal citizenship; Muslims don't want to change their religion as a condition for being accepted as equals. The relationship between class and citizenship lends itself to strategies that would *eliminate* the difference in order to achieve the equality – it turns our attention to ways of reducing or eliminating the impact of class on our political arrangements, and usually considers this in terms of actually reducing class difference. These other differences – of sex, ethnicity, religion, language and so on – require us rather to reconsider the meaning of equality in the context of a plural society.

Two approaches

There are two serious positions that people adopt in response to such a requirement (I ignore the one that says it cannot see what all the fuss is about). The first draws on the classical principles of liberal democracy. It treats political equality as a matter of equalizing individuals' access to political participation and influence, but does not consider the wider ramifications of representing group concerns. Those who adopt this position may develop it in a pretty radical direction: arguing, for example, that political equality requires considerably more than removing the legal barriers; that genuinely equal opportunities and access depend on major social reforms that will remove the obstacles to equal participation; and that, as part of the transition to this bright new world, we must introduce measures of affirmative action. But even so, this argument stops short of recognizing specifically group interests and concerns. It focuses exclusively on individual rights and individual access, on the changes that may be necessary to equalize our political weight.

As applied, for example, to the under-representation of women in political life, this approach would argue for quota systems to ensure that men and women are put forward in equal numbers as candidates for equally winnable seats; it would combine this with policies aimed at a major restructuring of the relationship between paid and unpaid work, so that women no longer assume primary responsibility for the work of caring for others. I highlight this aspect, because it is widely argued that women's exclusion from the political domain is related to the sexual division of labour at home and in work, and the particular difficulties women then face in combining politics with what is already a 'double shift' in their jobs and their responsibilities at home. This is only one aspect, but just tackling this would already imply far more extensive social regulation than we currently allow: insisting, at a minimum, that all employers make provision for substantial maternity *and* paternity leave; that all employers – whether their workers are men or women – make available reduced working hours for those with caring responsibilities; that all employers – whether they are in the public or private sector, whether they employ manual or professional workers – permit career breaks, with a guaranteed right to resume your old job; and, most costly of all, that the level of income support for those who take time off work to care for the young, sick or old is high enough to ensure that both women *and* men will do this.

This is a pretty radical scenario, but it still operates within a classically liberal paradigm of ensuring equal opportunities and access. It says that women should have genuinely equal opportunities with men to become our political representatives, and it goes one important step further, with the argument for quota systems, to say that equal opportunities are not met until there is also an equal outcome. It does not, however, say that these women politicians will then 'represent' the interests of women – and indeed, as long as women are elected by constituencies that are made up of both women and men, we wouldn't want them to be speaking for women alone. It is an argument in terms of individual equality rather than articulating group concerns.[17]

The second approach to the issue of democratic equality in a plural society regards this as falling a long way short of what is necessary to achieve this end. The problem, after all, is not just equal access as equal individuals; it is also a matter of recognizing specifically group concerns. Think here of the example of language. Clearly citizens who do not speak the official language of the country they live in are at a tremendous disadvantage – both economically and politically – and resources must be made available – through the schools but also for adults – that will enable them to learn this language. This alone might be enough to ensure that no individual is denied her equal rights to political participation by virtue of her country of origin. But if we just leave it at that, we are denying the legitimacy of any concerns these citizens may have with retaining the vitality of their original language and culture. We are saying that they can have equal access, but not really equal status: or rather that they can get equal status by dissolving themselves into the dominant groups. There is no space here for the notion that *all* groups might have an equal claim on social resources for sustaining their identity as a group: that minority as well as majority groups have a right to retain their linguistic or cultural identity – a right to be equal though different. Both French- and English-speaking Canadians have won this right; so too have the Welsh in Wales; the issue of bilingual education for Asian children in Britain is regarded as far more contentious.

Or consider some of the current discussion over proposals for a Bill of Rights for Britain, which have frequently centred on the problems in handing over the powers of interpretation to the judiciary as it is presently constituted.[18] Even those most committed to this reform worry that the old white men who currently control the higher courts cannot be relied upon to represent – or even to comprehend – the full range of concerns and experiences and perspectives within our society. The

Canadian experience with a Charter of Rights and Freedoms is hardly encouraging in this respect: in one notable recent example, the Canadian Supreme Court struck down as unconstitutional the so-called rape-shield which had been introduced to protect women bringing an accusation of rape against cross-examination on their sexual history, judging that this could undermine the rights of the accused to a fair trial. In this case, the rights of the accused won out over the rights of those bringing the accusation – and, while these conflicts of rights are always terribly tricky, this looks uncomfortably like a failure to register the way that the cards have been stacked against women.

Those who campaign for a Bill of Rights for Britain will always acknowledge this problem, and usually argue that the introduction of a Bill of Rights should be combined with measures to reform and extend the basis for recruitment into the judiciary. But there is a difficulty here. Not only that it will take a long time for any such reforms to permeate through to the higher levels, but that, even if we could conceive of a supreme court that was composed equally of men and women, and whose ethnic mix reflected that of the society at large, we would hardly expect the individuals concerned to be making their judgements as 'representatives' of this or that sex, this or that ethnic community. If we are seriously concerned (as I think we should be) that our democracies address the competing perspectives of both dominant and marginalized groups, then perhaps we should be considering alternative forms of *explicitly* group representation? One proposal that emanates from America is that disadvantaged or marginalized groups should be provided with public funding to enable them to formulate their own policy initiatives, and that the policy-makers should then be obliged to take these views into account.[19] An alternative that has surfaced in Britain is that we should have an elected second chamber charged with responsibility for considering group rather than just party concerns, a body that might be elected on a different kind of basis, and might then have responsibility for scrutinizing legislative proposals to weed out favouritism towards dominant groups.[20]

These are difficult issues, on which we have as yet no political consensus, and even among those who will agree that there is a problem (who will agree, that is, that certain voices are going unheard, or that certain groups are being excluded from the decision-making process) there is considerable unease with proposals that seem to reinforce group identities and division. Though we often talk about the value of diversity and the way this enriches our culture, people remain reluctant to follow this through to any significant conclusions – we may tolerate the differences that don't much matter (like agreeing that Rastafarians can wear their dreadlocks to work) but are less ready to concede resources or significant levels of self-determination.

One point I would make here is that the parallels that are so commonly drawn (by myself as much as anyone) between the political exclusion of women and the political exclusion of other marginalized groups may be misleading – precisely because women are not a numerical minority. In the case of women, we might want to say that equality of participation is indeed the central goal: but that, once women make up half of all decision-making bodies, there would be no need for any additional medium for representing specifically women's concerns. In the case of groups that constitute a numerical minority, equality in *participation* may not be enough to deliver on equality in *representation*. One black judge on the US Supreme Court is fair enough as a 'mirror' of the number of black Americans; thirty Asian or Afro-Caribbean MPs might be fair enough as a 'mirror' of the ethnic mix in British society. These numbers may be fair, but they still add up to a rather token presence; we cannot be confident that these changes alone would ensure that issues of racial equality would then pervade political debate.

There are further points of contrast we could make between women and genuinely minority groups. First, that the very notion of 'a' women's perspective is part of what women have to contend with: women can and should be able to adopt as many different perspectives as they like without thereby ceasing to be women. Secondly, that women have had to contest precisely that notion of 'community' that has become part of the politics of other disadvantaged groups: women have frequently pointed out that *the* religious community, *the* ethnic community, *the* local community (*the* socialist fraternity)[21] tends to be represented by community leaders who do not speak to the concerns of the women within that community. Feminism has tended to take issue with an undifferentiated – therefore potentially coercive – community, and while sharing some sense of a common cause with minority communities who have also felt excluded from the political arena, has been uneasy with the ways in which community interests get defined. One recent example from Britain relates to the demand from many Muslims for grant-aided status for Muslim schools. On the one hand, it seems grossly unfair that citizens who are Anglican or Catholic or Jewish can send their children to state-funded religious schools, but that (at the time of writing) this possibility is denied to citizens who are Muslim. On the other hand, a number of women's groups have registered their concern over the kind of education that might be offered to girls in the context of a potentially fundamentalist Muslim school – and have tended to favour getting all religions out of the schools.[22]

These are, as I say, troubling questions, on which I myself have as yet reached no final conclusion. The argument for equality of participation seems to me unassailable, and that alone sets us quite a task for change. The further questions of what mechanisms, if any, might be desirable for specific representation of specifically group concerns or what resources, if any, might be appropriate for supporting minority groups, are far more tricky. Certainly the fledgling initiatives towards articulating group voices through local authority channels have thrown up as many problems as they have resolved, and too often seemed to encourage what I would call a politics of the enclave which locked people into very narrow and specific concerns. Meanwhile, when we look to the current furore on American campuses over the challenges to the 'canon' in higher education, it often seems as if this is a democratic initiative that is likely to be strangled at birth.

One of the more curious elements in this is that, in the resistance to the new 'politics of difference', people seem to be coming back to precisely that notion of 'a' common good that we were told was thoroughly out of date. Through the onslaughts of the 'realist' tradition, we were encouraged to abandon any notions of a common purpose or a general will, and recognize that in the heterogeneous societies of the modern world there can be no universally agreed values. But when faced with a new pluralism that more profoundly challenges our notions of a single political culture, there is a hasty retreat to what looks like an untheorized version of that older 'common good'. It is as if pluralism was OK as long as it remained the pluralism of relatively dispassionate interest groups – all competing for their own rather secular and material concerns – but becomes out of the question once it expresses more confident claims for democratic self-determination. I never completely gave up on my notion of a politics of common purposes, so there is some residual consistency in my own sense that we must develop a version of democratic equality that can recognize and represent group difference without thereby collapsing into the politics of the enclave. We have to take more seriously than in the past the political inequalities between the different groups that make up our societies: to put it at its minimum, we have to deal in some way with that dangerous sense of being excluded from what ought to be a shared political world. But we have to do this in a way that opens up rather than closing down dialogue, that does not require people to speak only from their own particular sub-group. The chances of achieving this, however, depend crucially on those older ideals of participation and discussion and debate. Failing substantial and sustained interaction between the different groups that make up a plural and unequal society, we will find ourselves propelled into an unhappy choice between one of two alternatives: either making do with an inegalitarian democracy that refuses *any* mechanisms for dealing with group difference and group exclusion; or else moving towards a fragmented democracy that locks people into the partial concerns of divided and perhaps hostile groups. The fears of the second currently serve to encourage people to stick by the first, but in doing so they paper over what are becoming major cracks in the surface of political equality. Neither of the options is satisfactory, and the only way to break out of this circle is to return to further exploration of what have been dismissed as utopian dreams. I began with the suggestion that the old agenda of active citizen participation in the formation of common concerns had given way to a new agenda of achieving democratic equality. I end with a heightened conviction that these more recent promises of political equality cannot be divorced from those earlier ideals.

Notes

1 The description comes from W. J. Mommsen, *The Age of Bureaucracy* (Oxford: Blackwell, 1974) p. 95.
2 Robert Michels, *Political Parties: A Sociological Study of the Oligarchical Tendencies of Modern Democracy* (New York: Free Press, 1962).
3 Joseph Schumpeter, *Capitalism, Socialism and Democracy* (London: Allen & Unwin, 1942).
4 Giovanni Sartori, *The Theory of Democracy Revisited: Part One: The Contemporary Debate* (London: Chatham House, 1987).
5 Ibid., pp. 164–5
6 Michael Sandel, 'The procedural republic and the unencumbered self', *Political Theory*, 12, 1 (1984), p. 93.
7 See Chapter 6.
8 Derek Heater, *Citizenship: The Civic Ideal in World History, Politics and Education* (London: Longman, 1990), p. 4.
9 It is of course a major premise of Carole Pateman's work on consent that the detachment from masculinity is far from complete. See especially *The Sexual Contract* (Cambridge: Polity, 1988).

10 This same unprincipled pragmatism helps explain why, in the British campaign for women's suffrage, leaders of the Conservative Party lent a more sympathetic ear than leaders of the Liberal Party, despite the greater sympathy among rank and file Liberals for the principle of women's right to vote.

11 Francis Fukuyama, *The End of History and the Last Man* (London: Hamish Hamilton, 1992); Alan Ryan, 'Professor Hegel goes to Washington', *New York Review of Books* (26 March 1992); Jean François Revel, *How Democracies Perish* (New York: Harper and Row, 1983).

12 See, for example, Christopher Pierson, 'Democracy, markets and capital: are there necessary economic limits to democracy?', *Political Studies*, 40 (1992).

13 Most notably T. H. Marshall's work on citizenship. See his *Citizenship and Social Class and Other Essays* (Cambridge: University Press, Cambridge, 1950).

14 For example, Sidney Verba and Norman Nie, *Participation in America* (New York: Harper & Row, 1972); and Sidney Verba, Norman Nie and Jae-on Kim, *Participation and Political Equality: A Seven Nation Comparison* (Cambridge: Cambridge University Press, 1978).

15 Robert A. Dahl, *Democracy and its Critics* (New Haven, CT: Yale University Press, 1989).

16 See the work by Thomas Byrne Edsall and Mary D. Edsall, *Chain Reaction: The Impact of Race, Rights and Taxes on American Politics* (New York: Norton, 1991).

17 This is broadly the position I have argued myself in relation to the representation of women, feeling that the case can be quite adequately presented in terms of political equality or justice without getting into the more troubled waters of representing group interests and concerns. See Chapter 5.

18 Ronald Dworkin, *A Bill of Rights For Britain* (London: Chatto & Windus, 1990).

19 Iris Marion Young, *Justice and the Politics of Difference* (Princeton, NJ: Princeton University Press, 1990).

20 K. D. Ewing and C. A. Gearty, *Democracy or a Bill of Rights?* (London: Society of Labour Lawyers, 1991).

21 See ch. 1.

22 This is the position adopted by the secular group Women Against Fundamentalism, which was launched in 1989 to challenge the rise of fundamentalism in all religions. Its literature is available from BM Box 2706, London WC1 3XX.

8

Pluralism, Solidarity and Change

In the catalogue of revisions and recoveries that describes contemporary radical thought, few items stand out so starkly as the new attitude towards plurality and difference. The themes associated with difference have become particularly fashionable – as evidenced in various strands of feminist and post-modernist thought – and it would seem that pluralism has also redeemed itself. Paul Hirst's book on *Representative Democracy and its Limits* contains a chapter explicitly devoted to the retrieval of pluralism;[1] a recent collection on *Dimensions of Radical Democracy* is ordered around the project of a 'radical and plural democracy';[2] contemporary work in political philosophy positively groans under the weight of diversity, plurality and difference. Out of favour for many years, pluralism is now being yoked to its radical opposite as a kind of anti-establishment, anti-conformism: registering our refusal to pretend we are the same.

This marks a major shift in attitude. Through much of the preceding decades, pluralism served as a warning sign to all good radicals, who would then gather themselves up to do battle against its complacent defence of the status quo. In the world of political theory, for example, pluralism was closely associated with attacks on the excesses of utopian thinking – linked with Karl Popper's contrast between the open and the closed society,[3] or with Isaiah Berlin's contrast between negative and positive freedom.[4] Pluralism took issue with any tradition of political thought that looked towards the perfectibility of the human condition, and its practitioners identified a dangerous utopianism or more drastic totalitarianism in all such grandiose ideals.

Marxism was a common object of these critiques, but so too was any body of theory that offered a model of the good society. Much

Enlightenment thinking, for example, had conceived of a unified and unifying morality that was in principle available to rational enquiry, and, while acknowledging the wide range of beliefs and values currently embraced by different nationalities or cultures, tended to regard these as stages in historical development that would ultimately arrive at one identical point. While contesting many aspects of Enlightenment thinking, Marxism shared this expectation of future convergence. Thus Marx and Engels anticipated a process of historical development which would reduce and eventually eliminate the significance of divisions by race, sex, religion, nationality – which would 'batter down all Chinese walls' and make 'national one-sidedness and narrowmindedness become more and more impossible',[5] which would forge a common humanity in the context of a classless society. Both traditions looked forward to a future transcendence of division and distinction, believing that what now appears as fundamental difference will turn out as mere phases in development and progess.

The key theorists of pluralism had no time for such delusions. Against what they saw as the utopian modelling of wild-eyed dreamers, they stood for the more modest trial and error of 'piecemeal social engineering'. Against the dangerous despotism of any one vision of the social good, they argued the irreconcilability of different systems of value and the necessary pluralism of moral ideals. The arguments were all on the side of moderation, and, for those who felt themselves tussling with the injustices and inadequacies of present societies, the easy accusations of 'utopianism' or 'totalitarianism' seemed a route to political passivity. Pluralism equalled scepticism; scepticism led to a terrible failure of imagination. The philosophers of pluralism were abandoning all hopes for the future just because of some risks that might accompany change.

The kind of pluralism that developed in political science or political sociology took a different form, but here too it gained itself a sorry reputation as apologetics for the status quo. Generations of students were introduced to the divide between pluralism and Marxism; countless essays were written querying the false complacencies of the first or the outdated simplicities of the second. As pluralism developed (particularly within American political science), it was perceived as a direct challenge to 'ruling class' or 'elite' theories of the state: an approach that stressed the dispersal rather than the concentration of power; that talked of the checks and balances exerted by competing interest groups; that implied all was well in contemporary democracy.

Radicals regarded this as poor analysis made even worse by its limited ambition. In stressing the complex differentiation of society into a variety of interest groups, pluralist theory was thought to underplay – indeed deny – the more fundamental binary divide between classes. In conceiving of democracy as adequately safeguarded by the presence of multiple elites, it was said to gloss over systematic and sustained inequality. In accepting a vision of politics as activated solely through group interest, it was said to legitimate a sordid particularism in which no group looked beyond its own private and material advantage. Pluralism seemed to be telling us that our own sense of democratic impotence was irrelevant so long as it was sufficiently shared, and that human beings were not made for solidarities any wider than the group. Radicals argued forcefully against each point.[6]

The gulf was often based on mutual misrecognition, but this was hardly – at the time – to the point. Robert Dahl, for example, was frequently (and correctly) cited as a leading exponent of pluralist theories of democracy, but it was rarely perceived that 'the theorist in question, far from being a died-in-the-wool reactionary, is far to the left of the American political spectrum'.[7] Critics of Dahl largely passed over his own *Dilemmas of Pluralist Democracy*,[8] which explicitly acknowledged many of the problems that preoccupied the left: the way that pluralism can reinforce and sustain inequalities in the distribution of political resources; the way it can deform civic consciousness by strengthening particularistic over general concerns; the way it can distort the public agenda by excluding alternatives that speak to the needs of unorganized groups; the way it weakens the control of elected representatives over the machinations of wayward sub-groups. More significantly still (for anyone can recognize a problem without feeling called upon to offer solutions), the solutions Dahl proposes have long included a commitment to reducing economic inequality, increasing workplace democracy, and moderating the impact of the market. Whatever disagreements remain between Dahl and his critics on the left (and these are not insignificant), no one reading the latest restatement of his views on democracy would want to dismiss him as apologist for the status quo.[9]

Dahl's position on the political spectrum is now more precisely delineated by those who discuss pluralist theories of democracy, and this retrieval is itself symptom of a larger development. The deep gulf between pluralism and the left is being bridged, and part of the background to this convergence lies in the realm of political sociology and the increasingly subtle revisionism Marxism had to practise in order to cope with the absence of a clear ruling class. In the course of the 1970s and 1980s, Marxist or Marxist-influenced radicals distanced themselves from what they now regarded as the 'vulgar' Marxism of an earlier period. The notion of a simple binary divide between capital and labour lost much of its appeal, as did functionalist analyses of the relationship between class and the state. European Marxists proposed modified forms of class analysis that would accommodate the 'new middle class', experimented with different ways of identifying class 'fractions' or layers, or exposed the lack of unity and cohesion within the so-called capitalist class.[10] The dominance of class itself was challenged through the work of feminists, who proposed new theories of patriarchy or the sex/gender system, and developed alternative analyses of the basis of oppression and the formation of political identity.[11] The quintessentially Marxist notion of class as a simplifying and unifying dichotomy came to be seen as an extrapolation without historical foundation. Class unity, it was claimed, never did override sexual, national, religious or ethnic division. It was simply perverse to seek to explain male power over women or the rise of fascism or the brutalities of racism without reference to non-class forces.

These revisions already shifted the focus of analysis towards a more plural understanding of social division and political forces, but it is developments in the realm of normative political thought that have brought about the final recuperation. Particularly important here is the increased insistence on a multiplicity of perspectives and values: a growing recognition that, while individuals may and do change their beliefs and values, there is nothing that guarantees convergence over some basic or unifying concerns. Obvious as this has long seemed to those espousing a pluralist philosophy, it reached wider acceptance among radicals only with the recent challenges to modernist thought. The last decades have brought with them a major crisis of confidence in modernist thinking – a massive onslaught on Enlightenment ideals. Some of the pressure comes from those who seek their inspiration in pre-Enlightenment traditions;[12] more of it from those who look beyond the Enlightenment to explore what is increasingly described as post-modernism.[13] A significant contribution comes from feminist theory, which in exploring the masculine bias of universalizing theory has ended up endorsing much of the post-modern critique.[14]

A dominant tradition in contemporary political thought now stresses contingency, contestation and change. Richard Rorty has approached this through an anti-foundationalism that removes the authority from supposedly fundamental humanist ideals;[15] John Keane has approached it through a democratic relativism that refuses any undisputed truth;[16] William Connolly has approached it by exploring the 'essentially contested nature' of all the most basic political concepts.[17] The examples are in some sense arbitrary, for the mood they indicate is so widely shared that almost any examples would do. In each case, the arguments remove the basis for either an existing or a future consensus. A plurality of convictions is seen as both inevitable and permanent, and those who present this plurality as a mere passing phase are felt to be on dangerous ground. In terms already familiar from the arguments of earlier pluralists, today's theorists warn against the illicit imposition of one view as if it were the only and necessary truth.

The implication – for example, in Rorty's work – is not that we must give up on our most cherished beliefs, more that we should recognize their status as beliefs that are valid for ourselves. The corollary, of course, is that others may hold very different beliefs with equal legitimacy and conviction, and that there is no final reference point in either logic or history that will resolve potential dispute. This broadly relativist position has been around for many years, but events of the past decades have helped shift the balance more fully in its favour. Consider here the growing importance of Islam in world politics, which has forced Western intellectuals to reconsider the tensions between a secular humanism and religious modes of thought. Or think of the grotesque consequences of a socialism that anticipated the ending of 'significant difference' by refusing to permit variation, and threatened in the process the very validity of socialist ideals.[18] Whether we welcome the ensuing relativism or not, few would now want to be associated with a politics that refuses to recognize alternatives, or claims to know the solutions in advance.

This 'moral pluralism' has coincided with the second major element in contemporary pluralist thinking: the growing distrust of monolithic solutions. As socialists came to terms with the crisis and collapse of the centralized economies, those who were not already there moved towards some version of a 'mixed' economy – arguing for a combination of state enterprises, co-operative enterprises and small scale private enterprises,[19] and refusing the either/or conflict between the market and the plan.[20] Much the same pattern has characterized recent re-thinking on the nature and development of democracy. There is by now a virtually unanimous consensus on the importance of multi-party competition, and the main defining feature of radical democracy is that it presses for still more diversity. Thus John Keane calls for a 'plurality of democratic public spheres' in which different groups of citizens could participate if they so wished;[21] while David Held develops a 'principle of democratic autonomy' that will increase the range of circumstances in which citizens make the decisions for themselves.[22] These arguments add up to more than a defence of local democracy against a bureaucratic centre, for what they emphasize are the multiple avenues through which people will choose to exercise their autonomy and control, and the necessary and desirable variation. Stanislaw Ehrlich once defined pluralism as 'that trend which strives to restrict centralism . . . which opposes uniformity, both in social and political structure and in the sphere of culture'.[23] This refusal of uniformity is very much part of the new pluralism. Politics cannot and should not be standardized; there can be no one set of answers to all anticipated and unforeseen problems.

The final element in the recuperation of pluralism – and this is the one that comes closest to the mainstream tradition in political science – is the growing emphasis on the political significance of sub-groups that are defined through gender, ethnicity, religion, disability, sexuality, language and so on. This development has been very much informed by the emergence and theorization of the so-called new social movements, whose point of reference has been identities other than class.[24] How new these movements are remains a moot point (which I shall not try to resolve), but they have certainly achieved a novel impact on the development of left theory. As recently as the 1960s and 1970s, radicals still tended to regard forms of political mobilization that were based around ethnicity, gender or sexuality as politically immature: early moments in consciousness, not yet dignified by the discovery of class. Since then, the declining vitality of an explicitly class politics has combined with the sustained energy of these alternative social movements to encourage a more positive assessment of their role; and this shift in emphasis has been much enhanced by the fact that today's radicals are largely 'products' of one or other social movement. In drawing out the implications of this new politics, people have distanced themselves still further from the binary simplicities of an earlier age. They have come to speak far more confidently of the value to be attached to heterogeneity, diversity and difference.[25]

A new politics of difference has therefore emerged that emphasizes the multiple bases for political identity, and no longer considers these as stages en route to a unified working class. The break with class was just the first part of this process, and the pluralism has been radical and continuous. Many have noted, for example, how the initial unity of the women's movement dissolved under the weight of differences between women, and how the first challenge to the simplicities of class swept feminism almost inexorably into a later challenge to the simplicities of 'woman' or 'women'. As Susan Bordo observes, feminist criticism had barely begun its work on the false universals of male theory before turning its attention 'to its own narratives, finding them reductionist, totalizing, inadequately nuanced, valorizing of gender difference, unconsciously racist, and elitist.'[26] The working class was a false unity imposed over divisions between women and men; but so too was women a false unity, imposed over differences between white women and black, heterosexual and lesbian, first world and third world, Jewish, Muslim and atheist. Multiple differences have become the focus of the day.

Pluralism and solidarity

The pluralism in these new developments is considerably more radical than the mainstream pluralism it echoes, but part of the problem I want to consider is that, where it is more radical, it is also more disruptive of traditional solidarity. As already noted, one recurrent complaint levelled against mainstream pluralist theory was that it glossed over systematic political inequality. Celebrating the dispersal rather than the concentration of power, it failed to come to terms with the sustained exclusion of marginal groups from any kind of power at all. The new pluralism can hardly be held to account for this same failing: on this point at least, it can take pride in breaking new ground. Many exponents of the new pluralism have explicitly concerned themselves with identifying and empowering hitherto marginalized groups, stressing the inequalities that regulate relations between different social or cultural groups, and proposing new forms of democracy that can validate and empower people as members of their specific social groups. Far from disparaging the group basis of such mobilizations (as in a century of socialist distaste for women's self-organization as women) such theorists treat social heterogeneity as both necessary and positive. Far from ignoring systematic social inequality (as in the blander versions of mainstream pluralism) such theorists will support the self-organization of women, of black people, of disabled people, of lesbians and gay men; will encourage caucuses of such groupings within whatever organizations they find themselves; and, in the most fully developed versions, have called for new democratic procedures that will ensure additional representation for all oppressed groups.[27] This is a pro-active, not a laissez-faire pluralism. It therefore escapes the standard critique of the older pluralism that it attaches insufficient weight to the problems of political equality.

But then, precisely because of this, it leaves itself more exposed to the other critique: that, in conceiving politics as a matter of competition between groups (each pressing for its own advantage), pluralism has abandoned any hope of common or unifying concerns. Theorists of the older pluralism happily rejected what they saw as the outmoded, or always inappropriate, politics of a common interest: arguing (as did Joseph Schumpeter)[28] that there is no such thing as a common good; or, more interestingly (as does Robert Dahl), that such notions had meaning only in the context of smaller and more homogeneous societies.[29] The absence of any over-arching forms of social cohesion gave no particular cause for concern, partly because this pluralism was premised on interest rather than identity groups. Exponents of pluralist democracy typically conceived of people as mobilized around a variety of temporary concerns: politically passive for most of their lives; paper members, perhaps, of a number of overlapping associations or pressure groups; springing into occasional and temporary action only under exceptional conditions, when they perceived their interests as directly under threat. In such a scenario, it hardly mattered that people's loyalties and solidarities were restricted to a locality or a group. Most people were thought to have a number of associations or interests, none of which was all-embracing or dominant, few of which were intensely felt. Where political mobilization follows this pattern, democracy may well remain tolerant and stable. The relative apathy of the constituent groups is enough to keep the society firmly on the road.

This kind of argument is less readily available to the exponents of the new pluralism. Because these make more serious claims in terms of empowering previously marginalized voices – because they are more radically egalitarian in their aims – they are also more vulnerable to criticism for encouraging division and fragmentation. The new pluralism homes in on identity rather than interest groups: not those gathered together around some temporary unifying concern – to defend their neighbourhood against a major road development, to lobby their representatives against some proposed new law – but those linked by a common culture, a common experience, a common language. These links are often intensely felt, and, more important still, are often felt as opposition and exclusion. Identity groups frequently secure their identity precisely around their opposition to some 'other', focusing on a past experience of being excluded, and sometimes formulating a present determination to exclude.

In both Britain and the USA, for example, there was a period in which black and white activists worked together in anti-racist organizations and activities, in what the white activists at least perceived as relatively untroubled alliance. The development of a more assertive identity politics disrupted this relationship, bringing with it a critique of assimilationism and a repudiation of white 'liberal' support. As long as the politics was premised on shared ideas – of combatting racism, securing civil rights, promoting racial equality – then the key qualification for membership remained commitment to these ideas. But growing resentments over the continuing importance of white people within such organizations, combined with an increasingly confident sense of cultural and ethnic identity among black people, shifted the focus towards identities rather than ideas. From that point onwards, it began to matter immensely whether you organized autonomously as members of the same ethnic group, what kinds of alliances you struck with people from other ethnic groups, and which groups dominated the leadership roles within your organization.

Likewise in the history of feminism, most of the major campaigns through the nineteenth and twentieth centuries allowed a subordinate but supporting role to men who shared the campaigning ideals. Men were not expected to provide much of the energy or membership or action (just as well, for they didn't) but few feminists of the earlier era would have turned down an offer of financial or political support. As the contemporary women's movement developed through the 1960s and 1970s, it adopted a more explicitly separatist line. The few early meetings at which 'like-minded' men and women met together to discuss sexual equality fell all too readily into a familiar pattern of male dominance, and feminists moved swiftly to an organizational autonomy that excluded the participation of men. In this case, of course, most women still worked or lived with the 'other'. But this only heightened the tensions that were to emerge between those who extended their identity politics into a fully separatist life style and those who sought to maintain a more middle ground. Numerous comments by 1970s and 1980s feminists testify to the added intensity of this identity-based politics. Disagreements that might have been just about manageable if they had remained in the realm of alternative policies and ideas became virtually impossible to cope with when translated into identity terms.

In the case of Britain, the tension over sexuality and separatism contributed substantially to the collapse of a unified women's movement at the end of the 1970s, and, though these tensions never reduced to a simple divide between heterosexual and lesbian feminists, the shift from an ideas-based to a more intensely identity-based politics was an important part of the phenomenon. This shift also brought with it a wider fragmentation around multiple differences between women, with divisions around ethnicity or religion or nationality adding to the long-felt tensions around class. Through much of the 1970s, feminists had defined themselves along an essentially ideological spectrum of liberal versus radical versus socialist feminisms, and, while the disagreements between each 'school' were often deeply felt and strongly argued, they remained within a broadly shared consensus of seeking out the main causes of women's oppression.[30] By the end of the 1970s, this ideas-based categorization had shifted towards a range of more identity-based divisions. While it would be seriously misleading to suggest that feminists then arranged themselves into different sub-groupings ordered by class or ethnicity or sexuality or age, the changing basis of feminist identity and fragmentation proved less amenable to continued shared debate.

Consider, for example, the recent experience of the National Women's Studies Association, which was set up in the United States in 1976 to bring together women concerned with the development of women's studies. From its origins, this body encapsulated many of the assumptions of the new pluralism. It recognized, for example, that women were not a homogeneous category, and it developed a complex series of democratic mechanisms that would empower minority points of view. Broadly, this has taken the form of 'official caucuses', which can be formed by any sub-group that establishes a case for additional representation. This might be on the grounds that the group is made up of women who are particularly and additionally oppressed within the wider society (thus women of colour, lesbians, poor and working-class women); or it might be on the grounds that the group is one whose voice would not otherwise be sufficiently heard within the Association (teachers, for example, of pre-kindergarten to twelfth-grade students). The recognized caucuses are then entitled to their own delegates on the policy-making bodies: since members have representation through their regions as well as their caucuses, those attached to caucuses therefore enjoy additional representation.

In a recent study of this experience, Robin Leidner describes it as embodying a tension between individualist liberal democracy – which finds expression in the procedures of one person, one vote – and corporatist representation of groups – which pursues a different version of equalizing weight.[31] She notes that the resulting pattern of representation gave cause for concern among some of the women associated with university women's studies programmes, who felt the original intent of the organization had been shifted in a direction that no longer met their needs. These argued for and then formed their own caucus. Through most of the 1970s and 1980s, the overlapping membership of the different caucuses combined with the solidaristic sense of being involved in a common endeavour to keep divisive pressures at bay. But the procedures of caucus representation only worked to the extent of getting different issues on the agenda; they did not contain any further mechanisms for resolving potential disputes. In 1990, after a series of arguments over institutional racism, the caucus of African-American women left the association to establish a separate organization.

The formation of caucuses can help change the composition of those who participate in an organization, and thereby broaden the range of issues that are addressed. Failing resolution of these issues, however, caucuses also tend to sharpen the intensity of disagreement. In her version of events, Leidner suggests that members of the association found it hard to distinguish between 'equal power' and 'equal satisfaction': that, in creating a mechanism for establishing an equal voice to groups that would otherwise be marginal, the association heightened expectations that minority priorities would then get equal weight. But 'the expectation of equal satisfaction is a radical one, usually met only by schism. It is unlikely that such an expectation can be met within a heterogeneous democratic organization.'[32] Equal power is one thing – and given the inequalities of either society or organization may well dictate additional representation to minority groups. Equal satisfaction for both minorities and majorities is simply impossible – except in the exceptional circumstances where 'the majority wholly identify the interests of the minorities as their own'.[33] Such exceptions do occur, but rarely for long. Serious division and fragmentation become far more probable within a pluralism that sets out to empower each minority voice.

This is part of the problem I want to address. Insofar as radicals concern themselves (as they surely should) with the unequal distribution of power and influence, they have to consider group difference and group identity as a legitimate basis for political organization. They have to acknowledge, that is, the importance of autonomous organization for groups that perceive themselves as disadvantaged or oppressed. They have to consider the role of caucuses in strengthening the voice of such groups, and explore the forms of additional representation that might be required to deliver an equality of power. But in doing this, they may be validating an exclusive and fragmented politics that leaves little space for the development of a wider solidarity. The politics that develops from this may block future alliances for change. The retrieval of pluralism thus presents radicals with a problem that does not figure for their mainstream precursors, for the problem of solidarity arises only in traditions that deal in prospects for change. The political context out of which the new pluralism has emerged (socialist, feminist, anti-racist, etc.) is one that necessarily concerns itself with the conditions under which people join together in common cause over common oppressions, and is rightly preoccupied with those circumstances that will generate alliances for change. The kinds of questions posed by such radicals recurrently return to this ground. What is it that enables people to see beyond the specificities of their own life (each one unique in its own way) towards what might be shared experiences and goals? What kind of ideas or experiences promote this? What is likely to get in its way?

Solidarity has long been conceived as the opposite of difference: something that develops when and because difference disappears. The new pluralism has little time for this older teleology of transition, encouraging a far more positive celebration of what earlier activists had considered partial or parochial or lesser. But as far as prospects for solidarity are concerned, this more celebratory notion of group difference looks considerably less hopeful. Instead of seeking out some common ground with those who are like us only in parts of their identity, or discovering our own limits and partialities in the recognition of other points of view, we may find ourselves propelled towards a more exclusionary assertion of precisely what makes us different. It is hard to see the bases for wider solidarity in this.

This is a problem that has increasingly preoccupied me, and I want to approach it here from two different angles, both of which may push the discussion further along. The first involves considering the only tradition in mainstream pluralism that has seriously engaged with identity politics, and identifying what can be learnt from this. I have noted that most theories of pluralist democracy deal with interest-based – or perhaps ideas-based – groups, and do not consider the additional plurality of groups whose association arises from a common culture or a common identity. The major exception to this is consociationalism, a

term developed by Arendt Lijphart to describe the institutional practices of those European countries that have been characterized by
linguistic and religious division. What lessons, if any, can be learnt from
this tradition? What light does it cast on the problems of group difference
and solidarity?[34]

In the second section, I turn to discussions of tolerance and justice,
considering Susan Mendus's discussion of *Toleration and the Limits of
Liberalism*[35] and Iris Young's recent discussion of 'Justice and communicative democracy'.[36] In both cases the emphasis is on validating
difference, but within a public arena that can encourage interaction and
change. I raise here what may prove to be a particularly difficult issue,
relating to the asymmetry between dominant and subordinate groups.
If one of the values in recognizing difference is that it obliges dominant groups to reconsider the partiality of their own position, is there
an equal injunction on subordinate groups to reconsider their own
perspectives?

Consociationalism

The most obvious point of comparison between consociationalism and
the new pluralism is that consociational democracy – later redescribed
as 'consensus democracy' – deals in group divisions of a non-class
nature. Arendt Lijphart sets out to consider the problems of democracy
in plural societies that are characterized by 'segmental cleavages' of
'a religious, ideological, linguistic, regional, cultural, racial or ethnic
nature'.[37] He addresses, that is, some (though by no means all) of the
group divisions that are highlighted in the new pluralism.

His fundamental starting point is that patterns of majoritarian rule
are inappropriate to such societies. The winner-takes-all principle (most
graphically exemplified in the electoral systems of Britain and the USA)
ensures the dominance of the party that captures the largest single share
of the votes; and, while this principle may be perfectly acceptable in a
society that enjoys a recurrent see-saw between two competing parties,
it is both undemocratic and dangerous in a plural society that contains
'virtually separate subsocieties with their own political parties, interest
groups, and media of communication'.[38] The problem is not so much
that majoritarianism excludes minority *opinions*, for most people will
accept it as part of the working principles of democracy that the policies

preferred by a majority should take precedence over policies that have only minority support. The problem arises when these differences of opinion coincide with more fundamental communal differences that have locked people into their own 'subsociety' and discouraged association between different groups. In such cases, each minority remains permanently a minority, while each majority remains securely in power. Thus Catholics in Northern Ireland will not vote for Unionist parties, nor Protestants for the Social Democratic Labour Party or Sinn Fein. Where party preferences so consistently follow communal divides, the larger community has the permanent political advantage.

One frequent (and by no means disreputable) response is to look to such social or educational or political developments as might break down entrenched barriers between communities, arguing that this will then shift the grounds of political division onto less troubled – but perhaps more 'substantial' – terrain. Thus in Northern Ireland there are repeated – if very minority – ventures into 'mixed' schooling or 'mixed' youth clubs, and, on the political level, there is a recurrent debate over whether the main political parties in Britain should contest elections in Northern Ireland. Those who favour this argue that political choices would then move beyond the predominantly religious divide, and that, in forging common ground over social and economic policy, the Catholic and Protestant communities would be able to address what are by implication the more substantive problems in their lives. Inside the British Labour Party, a major counter-argument has been that this would involve recognizing the partition of Ireland as a final, irreversible fact, for it would mean treating the Northern counties of Ireland as simply part of a united UK. From Lijphart's perspective, the more crucial counter-argument is that integration is just wishful thinking. 'The integration of a deeply divided society may not be possible at all and certainly cannot be achieved in a reasonably short time.'[39] Where this is so, the real choices will come down to either power-sharing between divided communities, or else partition along subcultural lines.

There are two things to note here, both of which limit the relevance of consociationalism to the more general problems I raised earlier. The first is that Lijphart and others have concerned themselves only with those group divisions which are *already* activated in politics, or those that will be activated as soon as there is freedom to form political parties. The basic framework of consociational theory is set by the issue of stability, and the question is not how to empower groups that have been exluded from politics, but how to deal with those who have generated their own political organizations. Lijphart makes the point even more narrowly, arguing that the clue by which we recognize a significant segment is whether or not it produces its own political party.

One of the tests of whether a society is genuinely plural is whether or not its political parties are organised along segmental lines. We can turn this logic around: if we know that a society is plural, but cannot identify the segments with complete confidence, we can take our cue from the political parties that form under conditions of free association and competition.[40]

If these conditions are met, then any segment that is significant enough to make a legitimate claim to a share of the power will make this known by forming its own political party. If it fails to do so, we can assume that it is not a significant segment.

This is compelling enough if all one cares about is stability (why make things more difficult by identifying groups that have not bothered to identify themselves?) but then has little to say on the issue of equality between different groups. Because it deals only with the enabling conditions of free association and competition, it does not tackle the corrosive consequences of powerlessness and marginalization, and the ways these can inhibit the development of any group identity that differs from the dominant norm. And because it sets the stakes so high, requiring of groups not only that they have a strong sense of themselves and their own interests but that they form their own political party as well, it excludes from consideration most of the groups that figure in arguments of the new pluralism. (Consider, by contrast, Iris Young's tentative list for contemporary America: 'women, blacks, Native Americans, Chicanos, Puerto Ricans and other Spanish-speaking Americans, Asian Americans, gay men, lesbians, working class people, poor people, old people, and mentally and physically disabled people'.)[41] The most marginalized will be as marginal in a consociational democracy as they are anywhere else; neither the theory nor the practice is about equalizing democratic weight.

The second point to note is one repeatedly made in the literature: that consociationalism is not so much about democracy as about accommodation between political elites. The power-sharing mechanisms advocated by Lijphart and others depend crucially on the co-operation of political leaders, who work to moderate what might otherwise be explosive tensions between their respective communities. 'In a consociational democracy, the centrifugal tendencies inherent in a plural society are counteracted by the cooperative attitudes and behavior of the leaders of the different segments of the population.'[42] Deals are struck between these leaders in conditions of confidence and secrecy that conduce to political accommodation, and each leader undertakes to deliver the support of his segment for whatever the final deal. As one of the more vocal critics puts it: 'Consociation boils down in practice to a conservative cartel of ethnic elites sharing power by giving priority to their *class* over their ethnic interests. The success stories are few; the problems are many; and the democracy is largely a fiction.'[43]

In thinking about the lessons that can be drawn from the theory and practice of consociationalism, it is important to recognize that the elitism here is no accident, but built into the whole approach. The more divided the society, the more potentially explosive the tensions; but then the deeper the segregation, the more powerful will be each segment's elite. A group that is only loosely unified, across a range of overlapping – and perhaps conflicting – identities and interests, is likely to throw up competing leaderships, and this will undermine the conditions for consociational success. The most favourable conditions for a stable consociational democracy are those in which the leadership of each group has unchallenged authority – due to the internal cohesion of the segment itself, or more generally (as in Lijphart's first analysis of the politics of accommodation in the Netherlands) because of the deferential nature of the political culture. The greater the internal democracy of any specific community, the more likely it is that members will query the deal that their leaders have struck: and what the elites had considered a happy compromise between 'their' community and the others may fail to win enough popular support.[44]

Note one important consequence of this. Lijphart has argued – and, in his own terms, the argument is entirely coherent – that it does not matter if consociational devices shore up and strengthen divisions between segments. Since power-sharing will encourage the proportional distribution of resources and offices between the different segments, this will most likely increase social segmentation, and initially intensify the plural divisions. No problem, says Lijphart, for this potential increase in plural conflict will paradoxically enhance the chances for consociational success. If the sub-cultural identity becomes even more important in each individual's life, then the power and authority of the group's leaders will correspondingly increase, and it will be even easier to deliver the support of the followers en bloc. Internal democracy may diminish, fragmentation increase, any wider solidarity become a meaningless joke. As far as political stability is concerned, however, the chances will be better than ever. The bitterness and bigotry of group closure simply do not figure as issues in this, for they are considered compatible with a stable democracy.

Since elite power is part and parcel of the consociational theory of democracy, its maintenance is hardly viewed as a problem. And since the emphasis throughout is on stability rather than equality or change, there is nothing to worry about in the formation of exclusionary political identities which derive their force from seeing others as almost a species apart. As long as the leaders are sufficently immunized from this process to retain their spirit of accommodation, deals can be struck and stability ensured. The followers may become so immersed in segmental self-definition that they can no longer bear to live in the same neighbourhood with others who are different from themselves, but if this works to enhance the authority of those who speak for their community or group it will help rather than hinder the 'democracy'. Consociationalism can simply abdicate responsibility for shoring up sectional division, can simply refuse to recognize it as a problem.

If we approach the question from the angle of the new pluralism, the risks of group closure become that much more severe. No radical will favour forms of group representation that deliver power to an unquestioned authority: the spokespeople (usually spokes*men*) of each tightly knit and exclusive community. So if the new pluralism also works to intensify a closed and oppositional politics, based around the narrow self-perceptions of divided and competing groups, it does not have the escape route of elite moderation. One might think here of what has been the closest approximation to consociationalism in recent British politics: the initiatives developed by a number of (left) local authorities to enhance the political profile of previously marginalized groups. These experiments developed in the 1970s and 1980s, and were boosted by the example of the then radical – and since abolished – Greater London Council. The categories through which the relevant groups were identified were derived largely from the equal opportunities industry (thus ethnic minorities and women), and, in the absence of any democratic procedures through which a 'community' could elect its spokespeople, the 'community representatives' tended to be professional activists, known to or indeed working for the council.

As non-elected, and therefore non-accountable, spokespeople, these came to operate as what Harriet Cain and Nira Yuval-Davis call 'advocates' rather than 'representatives',[45] their power base depending on the council's continuing patronage and being able to win enough funding to satisfy the demands of their group. In this competition for funds, and even more acutely in proposals for reorganizing working practices inside council departments or the grant-aided sector, each group came to emphasize its own marginality and deprivation in opposition to others. Individuals from other groups came to be seen almost as expressions of 'abstract social categories':[46] fair game for competition and attack. In these instances, neither leaders nor followers were inclined to explore the common ground with associated groups; perhaps because everyone was marginal and no one had power, there was no basis even for elite co-operation.

The theory and practice of consociationalism thus clarifies the problems without offering useful solutions. The new pluralism has to think far more seriously than any of its mainstream counterparts about the way that group representation can entrench a politics of competitive exclusion; has to consider whether it is worth the candle to ditch the blander universalisms of the Enlightenment if this leads straight to the politics of the enclave. The new pluralism cannot resort (as do the theorists of mainstream pluralism) to a happy vision of groups that are at odds with one another on some issues, but still reach a compromise on others, because it wants to engage with the more intensely felt politics of excluded and identity-driven groups. Nor can it retreat (as do the analysts of consociational democracy) to an unflappable tolerance of group rigidity, because it must keep worrying away at the conditions that will generate change. Consociationalism represents a way of dealing with difference by keeping group members apart: an approach in which only the elite is required to tackle the 'other'. While this may achieve greater fairness in the distribution of resources between a society's constituent groups, it offers no route at all towards resolving issues of solidarity or change.

Tolerance, justice and difference

For those working within an explicitly radical framework, the emphasis has been rather different. In her discussion of liberal perspectives on tolerance, for example, Susan Mendus explores the limits of a 'live and let live' approach to difference, arguing that liberal theories come up against intractable problems in defining the legitimate scope for toleration. Some resolve this in a classically Enlightenment fashion, presuming (as did John Stuart Mill) that autonomy will promote moral progress and spiritual improvement, and that, given enough freedom of thought and action, individuals and groups will converge on the 'right' way of life. Most contemporary liberals seek to avoid this perfectionism by insisting on their neutrality between different beliefs and different ways of life. Mendus argues that, in all cases, moral preferences creep in.

The crucial contrast she then draws between liberal and socialist perspectives is that the former emphasize the private spaces within which difference can flourish, while the latter concern themselves with a more public process of generating a wider community. She argues that the first part of the socialist impetus towards tolerating difference is simply a pragmatic one, based on a clearer understanding than is common in the liberal tradition that people do not simply 'choose' their membership of sub-groups. Socialists will see personal ideals as alterable, but not simply the objects of choice, and, because of this strong sense of individuals as products of their circumstances, will find intolerance an inappropriate reaction. Mendus goes on, however, to argue that this pragmatic impetus towards toleration can be welded to a more positive moral account. Because socialists aspire to a sense of loyalty and belonging, 'they require both more and less toleration than do liberals':[47] more, because toleration is then a necessary component in the development of larger loyalties; less, because the kind of permissive toleration that simply lets people get on with their own business is not enough to generate the sense of belonging. Socialists are engaged on a moral quest for a wider community and solidarity, and members of sub-groups will never achieve the requisite sense of belonging if they are simply enjoined to carry on in their own private world. Nor, however, will they achieve this sense of belonging if they feel they are being asked to give up one identity in order to take on some other.

In contrast to consociationalism, the argument is explicitly premised on change. Mendus is rejecting that frozen tolerance of difference in which each community or sub-group just carries on in isolation from all others; she is thus implicitly rejecting consociational mechanisms which deal only in the 'fair' distribution of power between groups that will remain different and potentially hostile. She presents difference more as a challenge, something that challenges dominant groups to reassess their own values and perspectives, but also challenges subordinate and excluded groups to go beyond sectarian loyalties. The ultimate goal is a wider sense of belonging, which is why difference can be neither denied nor simply left as it is.

A recent paper by Iris Young develops a similar sense of the relationship between group difference and change. Here Young reiterates her case for specific representation for oppressed or disadvantaged groups, but puts it in the context of a discussion of justice and communicative democracy. Where the older pluralism of interest groups concerns itself only with the representation of *interests*, the communicative theory of democracy emphasizes a process of transformation and change. Decisions are arrived at, not through backstage pressure or the anonymous casting of votes, but through direct interchange and discussion. In the process, participants may move from a narrow conception of their individual or group self-interest towards a concern with justice: indeed in order to be taken seriously in any democratic discussion, 'a person must transform his or her claim from "I want" to "I am entitled to" and offer some justification of this claim'.[48]

In societies characterized by group division and inequality, the combined emphasis on discussion and group representation can be expected to transform the politics of dominant groups.

Group representation unravels the false consensus that cultural imperialism may have produced, and reveals group bias in norms, standards, styles and perspectives that have been assumed as universal or of highest value. By giving voice to formerly silenced or devalued needs and experiences, group representation forces participants in discussion to take a reflective distance on their assumptions and think beyond their own interests. When confronted with interests, needs and opinions that derived from very different social positions and experience, persons sometimes come to understand the limitations of their own experience and perspective for coming to a conclusion about the best policy for everyone. Coupled with the knowledge that the perspectives expressed by oppressed groups also carry a specific vote, and thus that they cannot be ignored if the whole body is to come to a decision, such enhanced communication best promotes just outcomes.[49]

In both arguments, the emphasis is on public interaction between different groups, and the ways that difference then encourages a process of self-reflection and change. But the real force of the argument lies in the way that difference can alter the perspectives of dominant groups: this is where it appears most unambiguously positive. In considering the cultural imperialism of Western traditions, or the patriarchal assumptions of Enlightenment thought, or just the more self-regarding narrowness of groups who have a current monopoly on resources and power, it is easy enough to regard enforced exposure to alternative perspectives as a positive development. If the confrontation with difference disrupts or undermines the unthinking certainties of dominant groups, then all to the good. We need not presume in advance that there is nothing of value in their beliefs or ideals – but we have good reason to expect them to be limited and partial and biased. In such contexts, difference can and should generate change, encouraging a reassessment of what may prove unfounded complacencies and forcing people to reconsider what may be false generalizations from a very limited base.

But what of the more recently and perhaps still tentatively formulated assumptions of what are still subordinate groups? A confrontation that may seem thoroughly desirable in respect of the previously unchallenged dominance of narrowly unrepresentative groups appears less straightforwardly progressive in respect of those who have barely edged their way onto the public domain. Are these too to be 'disrupted' and 'undermined' and 'forced' to think more widely than themselves? Or should we say that, where there is an existing asymmetry in power, there should also be an asymmetry in what is demanded? So perhaps men should have to confront their gender bias, but women shouldn't yet face this injunction? Perhaps white Americans should be exposed to criticism for referring only to the 'canon' of white Americans, but black Americans shouldn't yet be required to be equally even-handed? To deny the difference between dominant and subordinate groups is to fall back into the complacencies of the older pluralism, and most radicals would want to avoid that conclusion. Is the implication that difference should only work to 'challenge' what are dominant groups – inviting perhaps a more modest 'self-reflection' among those who remain outside the fold?

In one sense this is a false dilemma, for groups that feel themselves excluded in the current distribution of resources or power have usually adopted a language of entitlements or justice, knowing full well that they have no chance with the simpler assertions of 'I want'. To this extent, they are already in the business of communicating with others across the boundaries of difference, and are unlikely to need reminding that there are groups that are different from themselves.[50] The problem arises only where the mounting frustration among members of marginalized groups produces a more defiant sense of closure. Oppressed or marginalized or disadvantaged groups may then feel themselves propelled into a more exclusionary or separatist politics that simply refuses to recognize the concerns of those they feel have too long ignored their own.[51] Once this happens, dominant groups are only too happy to feel themselves absolved from the pressure to reassess their own behaviour and beliefs.[52] Group division can then rigidify in a pattern that lends itself to more consociational solutions. The prospects for cross-group communication diminish, and it seems that the best we can hope for is a fairer distribution of resources and power. This is not an outcome to be welcomed by anyone who looks towards transformation and change.

What this indicates to me is that a radical perspective on democracy and difference must start from, but cannot remain exclusively within, the project of political equality. The systematic inequalities between dominant and subordinate groups provide us with a major part of any radical agenda, and direct our attention to the kinds of mechanisms that might be necessary to deal with existing asymmetries in power. But whatever form these mechanisms take (thus quota systems to guarantee a fairer distribution of political representation, or official caucuses to increase a sub-group's political weight, or some other of a range of alternatives) these will only contribute to a wider sense of solidarity if they work within the assumption of transformation and change. The problem, after all, is not just how to achieve a fairer distribution of resources and power between groups we expect to remain hostile, or contemptuous of one another. The problem is how to generate that more comprehensive understanding that validates the worth of each group. If we had this already, we would not be discussing this problem: it is clearly an outcome dependent on change.

Despite my anxieties on the subject, it seems clear that no group can remain immune from this process. It may be more unambiguously satisfying to disrupt or undermine the complacencies of dominant groups, but the challenge must inevitably be mutual, to both dominant *and* subordinate groups. We might think here of the criticisms that a number of feminists have made of the move to celebrate femininity or female values: if the formation of masculinity is problematic, how can we be so confident that femininity is immune?[53] The oppressed have no monopoly on good behaviour; being a victim is not a guarantee of right. Groups necessarily exist in relationship to one another, and, whatever bias or partiality we perceive in one group, it is all too likely to be mirrored in some aspect of the opposing camp. It is in the nature of groups to be partial, and this applies whether they currently enjoy power or not.

What we can say, however, is that the process of mutual challenge is neither defensible nor very likely to happen without initiatives that tackle the asymmetry in power. Failing these, it does indeed seem inappropriate to call on subordinate or marginalized groups to adjust themselves to what may be the prejudices of those with more power, and failing these, it will be hard to impress on the dominant that they must listen to an opposing voice. In this sense, genuine and substantial political equality is the *sine qua non* of a plural society. For any radical, however, it is the beginning rather than the end of the project, for the ultimate goal remains the forging of common cause across the boundaries of difference. Exponents of the older pluralism can bask in a happy neutrality over the 'interests' their interest groups press: no need for criticism or judgement or future directions for change. Those immersed in the new pluralism cannot follow this same route: cannot rely on the live and let live maxim as a way resolving problems of difference, nor rest content with consociational procedures that may shelter each group from the process of mutual challenge and change. The intractability of difference should not be viewed as an intractability of *particular differences*, and in so far as each social group defines itself in relation (and often in opposition) to some other, its sense of itself is necessarily fluid and liable to be transformed. While difference must be recognized and equality guaranteed, none of the differences is set in stone.

It is important, however, that this more dynamic sense of differences as changing, recomposing, even dissolving, should not lead us to a new version of the older myths of homogeneity. Particular differences can and do go away; solidarities can and are forged across what looked like formidable barriers. This is not to say that difference *per se* will disappear, or that if we only work hard enough on our mutual understanding we will converge on some single set of shared ideals. What distinguishes a radical perspective on democracy is not its expectation of future homogeneity and consensus, but its commitment to a politics of solidarity and challenge and change.[54]

Notes

1 Paul Hirst, *Representative Democracy and its Limits* (Cambridge: Polity, 1990).
2 Chantal Mouffe (ed.), *Dimensions of Radical Democracy* (London: Verso, 1992).

3 Karl Popper, *The Open Society and its Enemies* (London: Routledge & Kegan Paul, 1945).

4 Isaiah Berlin, *Four Essays on Liberty* (Oxford: Oxford University Press, 1969). For a recent discussion of 'The pluralism of Isaiah Berlin', see Perry Anderson, *A Zone of Engagement* (London: Verso, 1992).

5 Karl Marx and Friedrich Engels, 'The Communist Manifesto' (1847), in D. McLellan (ed.), *Marxism: Essential Writings* (Oxford: Oxford Unversity Press, 1977), p. 24.

6 The literature is immense, but key contributions were P. Bachrach and M. S. Baratz, 'The two faces of power', *American Political Science Review*, 56, 4 (1962); G. Duncan and S. Lukes, 'The new democracy', *Political Studies*, 11, 2 (1963); and C. Pateman *Participation and Democratic Theory* (Cambridge: Cambridge University Press, 1970), esp. ch. 1.

7 Hirst, *Representative Democracy and its Limits*, p. 56.

8 Robert A. Dahl, *The Dilemmas of Pluralist Democracy: Autonomy v. Control* (New Haven, CT, and London: Yale University Press, 1982).

9 Robert A. Dahl, *Democracy and its Critics* (New Haven, CT, Yale University Press, 1989). For a left critique that sets out remaining and major areas of dispute, see Philip Green, 'Review essay of Robert Dahl's *Democracy and its Critics*', *Social Theory and Practice*, 16, 2 (1990). Meanwhile Perry Anderson identifies Dahl as one of those seeking to synthesize liberal and socialist traditions. See 'The affinities of Norberto Bobbio', in Anderson, *A Zone of Engagement*, p. 90.

10 See, for example, N. Poulantzas, *Classes in Contemporary Capitalism* (London: New Left Books, 1975); G. Carchedi, *On the Economic Identification of Social Classes* (London: Routledge & Kegan Paul, 1976); E. Olin Wright, 'What is middle about the middle class?', in *Analytical Marxism*, ed. J. Roemer (Cambridge: Cambridge University Press, 1986).

11 For an overview of these debates, see M. Barrett, *Women's Oppression Today* (2nd edn, London: Verso, 1988).

12 Alasdair MacIntyre is the main example of this. See his *After Virtue* (London: Duckworth, 1981); and *Whose Justice? Whose Rationality?* (Notre Dame, IN: University of Notre Dame Press, 1988).

13 For example, Richard Rorty, *Contingency, irony and solidarity* (Cambridge: Cambridge University Press, 1989).

14 See the essays collected in Linda Nicolson (ed.), *Feminism/Postmodernism* (London: Routledge, 1990); and ch. 3.

15 Rorty, *Contingency, irony and solidarity*.

16 John Keane, *Democracy and Civil Society* (London: Verso, 1988), ch. 7.

17 William Connolly, *The Terms of Political Discourse* (Oxford: Martin Robertson, 1983), esp. ch. 6.

18 This is particularly powerfully argued in A. J. Polan, *Lenin and the End of Politics* (London: Methuen, 1984).

19   See Alec Nove, *The Economics of Feasible Socialism* (London: Allen & Unwin, 1983).

20   David Miller, *Market, State and Community: Theoretical Foundations of Market Socialism* (Oxford, Calendon Press, 1989).

21   Keane, *Democracy and Civil Society*, p. xiii.

22   David Held, *Models of Democracy* (Cambridge: Polity, 1986), ch. 9.

23   Stanislaw Ehrlich, *Pluralism on and off Course* (Oxford: Pergamon Press, 1982), p. xi.

24   R. Dalton and M. Kuechler (eds), *Challenging the Political Order: New Social and Political Movements in Western Democracies* (Cambridge: Polity, 1990).

25   One of the best examples is Iris Marion Young, *Justice and the Politics of Difference* (Princeton, NJ: Princeton University Press, 1990).

26   Susan Bordo, 'Feminism, postmodernism, and gender scepticism', in *Feminism/Postmodernism*, ed. Linda Nicolson, p. 135.

27   Young, *Justice and the Politics of Difference*.

28   Joseph Schumpeter, *Capitalism, Socialism and Democracy* (London: Allen & Unwin, 1942).

29   Dahl, *Democracy and its Critics*.

30   See introduction by Michèle Barrett and Anne Phillips to Barrett and Phillips (eds), *Destabilizing Theory: Contemporary Feminist Debates* (Cambridge: Polity, Stanford, CT: Stanford University Press, 1992).

31   Robin Leidner, 'Stretching the boundaries of liberalism: Democratic innovation in a feminist organization', *Signs*, 16, 2 (1991).

32   Ibid., p. 287.

33   Ibid., p. 288.

34   In *Justice and the Politics of Difference*, Iris Young briefly notes the parallels between her own vision of group representation and the European experience of consociationalism, noting, however, that 'European models of consociational democratic institutions . . . cannot be removed from the context in which they have evolved, and even within them it is not clear that they constitute models of participatory democracy' (p. 191). See also Jane Mansbridge, *Beyond Adversary Democracy* (New York: Basic Books, 1980), for an exploration of consociational principles of equalizing political outcomes.

35   Susan Mendus, *Toleration and the Limits of Liberalism* (London: Macmillan, 1989).

36   Iris Marion Young, 'Justice and communicative democracy', in *Tradition, Counter-Tradition, Politics: Dimensions of Radical Philosophy*, ed. Roger Gottlieb (Philadelphia: Temple University Press, forthcoming 1993).

37   Arendt Lijphart, *Democracy in Plural Societies: A Comparative Exploration* (New Haven, CT: Yale University Press, 1977) pp. 3–4. The central theses of consociational democracy are developed in Lijphart's analysis of *The Politics of Accommodation: Pluralism and Democracy in the Netherlands*

(Berkeley: University of California Press, 1968); and subsequently refined through his *Democracies: Patterns of Majoritarian and Consensus Government in Twenty-One Countries* (New Haven, CT: Yale University Press, 1984). His study on *Power-Sharing in South Africa*, Policy Papers in International Affairs (Berkeley: University of California Press, 1985) proposes a consociational constitution for South Africa, and includes an extended discussion of his critics. See also Lijphart, 'Democratic political systems: types, cases, causes, and consequences', *Journal of Theoretical Politics* 1, 1 (1989).

38   Lijphart, *Democracy in Plural Societies*, p. 22.

39   Arendt Lijphart, 'The Northern Ireland problem: cases, theories, and solutions', *British Journal of Political Science*, 5, 1 (1975), p. 104. Lijphart does not discuss the issue of the British Labour Party, but reviews literature that has proposed integration as the only solution.

40   Lijphart, *Power Sharing in South Africa*, p. 68. I should point out that Lijphart makes this argument in order to pre-empt a prior racial classification of the segments.

41   Iris Marion Young, 'Polity and group difference: a critique of the ideal of universal citizenship', *Ethics*, 99 (1989), p. 261.

42   Lijphart, *Democracy in Plural Societies*, p. 1.

43   Pierre L. van den Berghe, 'Protection of ethnic minorities: a critical appraisal', in *Protection of Ethnic Minorities: Comparative Perspectives*, ed. Robert G. Wirsing (Oxford: Pergamon Press, 1981) p. 349.

44   This was a point that Brian Barry developed in his 'Political accommodation and consociational democracy', *British Journal of Political Science*, 5, 4 (1975), where he argues that divisions based on ethnic identity may be less amenable to consociational management than those based around religion, because the former do not provide the same undisputed authority basis for 'the' leaders.

45   Harriet Cain and Nira Yuval-Davis, 'The "equal opportunities community" and the anti-racist struggle', *Critical Social Policy*, 29 (1990).

46   Ibid., p. 21.

47   Mendus, *Toleration and the Limits of Liberalism*, p. 158.

48   Young, 'Justice and communicative democracy', forthcoming, 1993.

49   Ibid.

50   Thus, for example, those concerned with measures to increase the political representation of black Americans have noted that it is impossible to rely only on increasing their numbers: when a group is in a numerical minority, its chances of transforming the political agenda depend on securing broader coalitions with white liberals. See Rufus P. Browning, Dale Rogers Marshall and David H. Tabb (eds), *Racial Politics in American Cities* (New York and London: Longman, 1990); and Lani Guinier, 'Voting rights and democratic theory: where do we go from here?', in *Controversies in Minority Voting:*

The Voting Rights Act in Perspective, ed. Bernard Grofman and Chandler Davidson (Washington, DC: Brookings Institution, 1992).

51 Nancie Caraway explores one version of this in her recent discussion of black feminist theory in the USA. In their powerful critique of white racism in the women's movement, black feminists have sometimes additionally argued that black women have a privileged access to the truth, precisely because of their marginalized or oppressed condition. Caraway raises problems in the privileging of any perspective, and argues for the 'robust and healing structures of democratic political practices'. *Segregated Sisterhood: Racism and the Politics of American Feminism* (Knoxsville: University of Tennessee Press, 1991), p. 196.

52 Something like this seems to have happened in the arguments on American campuses over the content of the undergraduate curriculum: the so-called political correctness debate. There is an extraordinary level of indignation among those who feel their cherished traditions under attack from a wave of 'minority' charges; and, while I too hate to be attacked by students, I cannot but feel that the catalogue of inappropriate demands has been collated in order to absolve people from changing what they teach. There is a certain amount of bad faith in employing what may well be the closed dogmatism of one's critics as a way of evading responsibility for questioning and reviewing oneself. I am aware that I speak from the relatively safe harbours of British universities – but, whatever may be the 'excesses' of those currently challenging the canon, these should not serve to excuse myopic practices among dominant groups.

53 See Lynne Segal, *Is the Future Female?* (London: Virago, 1987).

54 I am indebted here to comments by Susan Mendus, some of whose formulations have crept into my revised version.

Index

Index compiled by Ann Barham